MOMENTS of WONDER

52 NEW

ENGAGING CHILDREN'S MOMENTS

MARK BURROWS

Moments of Wonder
52 New Engaging Children's Moments

ISBN 9781426735981
PACP00935689-01

11 12 13 14 15 16 17 18 19 20 - 10 9 8 7 6 5 4 3 2 1

MANUFACTURED IN THE UNITED STATES OF AMERICA

TaBLe oF Contents

Musings From Mark 4

Let's Do Something 9

The World Needs You
to Be You 12

Answering the Call 14

Wonderfully Made...................16

There Is Only Us 18

Doors 20

Nana's Visit 23

Change 25

Good Is What We Do 28

Opposite Day............................30

Witnesses 31

Things That Just Happen 33

Believe......................................35

Bunnies and Eggs at Church ..37

Which Way? 40

A Warm Welcome 42

The Creation 44

The Still, Small Voice 46

Walking to Emmaus 47

Serve...48

Jesus Calls 49

Adam and Eve..........................50

The Birth of Jesus 52

Light of the World....................54

Fill Us Up 56

Worth Remembering 59

A T-Shirt From Dad.................61

How Can I Keep
From Singing?.......................63

What Love Can Do 65

All We Need..............................67

A Child Shall Lead 69

Making Room 71

Making Christmas Last...........73

More Than Words 75

One Person of Faith 77

Breathe......................................80

The Good Book.........................82

What God Wants for Us 84

Friends......................................86

Making Popcorn 88

Following 90

Remember Your Baptism 91

Brick by Brick...........................93

Do We Have to Go
to Church?.............................95

Wolf..97

Hello in Many Languages 99

Priority List 101

Five Thousand 103

Hosanna 104

She's a Hero..............................106

Kazoos 108

W. I. T. H...................................110

Scripture Index........................112

MUSiNGS FROM MaRK...

Hello Friends! It's been nearly two years since my first collection of Children's Moments — **Wow Time** — came out. And I feel very fortunate to be able to share with you this newest collection — **Moments of Wonder**. Now, after doing a little simple math, you'll note that there are 52 Sundays in a year and 52 Children's Moments in this collection. But there have been over 104 Sundays since I started putting this collection together. What happened to those other 52+ Sundays, Mark? Didn't you lead children's moments on those Sundays too? Well, um, yes, I did. Let's just say that many of them aren't really what I'd call "fit for publication." I'll spare you the pain and head-scratching confusion of some of my biggest clunkers. But I will share with you some of the lessons I've learned from those times when I simply didn't have "it."

Rhetorical Questions: You'd think after several hundred children's moments I'd know better than to ask a rhetorical question. But do you think I've learned my lesson? (Oops, there's another one.) In fact, I try not to ask too many questions, period. No matter how obvious I think the one "right" answer is, the kids always surprise me. Here's a perfect example — On the first Sunday of the New Year our senior minister decided to preach a sermon on the Ecclesiastes 3 text about there being a time for everything. I decided to base the children's moment on the Aesop's fable, "The Ant and the Grasshopper." The moral of the fable is that there is a time to work and a time to play. "The Ant and the Grasshopper" involves the two title characters. At no point in the story did I mention any characters other than the ant and the grasshopper. Then I got to the point in the story where the ant heard a knock at the door. Rather than just saying who it was, I asked, "And do you know who it was?" (Keep in mind this was the first Sunday in January. Many families still had their Christmas trees up.) No sooner was the question out of my mouth than one child yelled out with excitement, "Santa Claus!" Okay, you saw that coming. I, sadly, did not. My rule of thumb is — When you ask honest people a question, you're going to get an honest answer whether it's the answer you're looking for or not.

Engaging versus Entertaining: In the example of "The Ant and the Grasshopper" (and Santa Claus) the adults were highly entertained. But that's not really the point, is it? What had been, up to that point, a fairly strong children's moment, devolved into an episode of "Kids Say the Darnedest Things." The adults may laugh at what I or the kids are saying and doing. They may even applaud at the end. But that doesn't mean I've done my job. I'm not there to entertain the grownups, and neither are the children. And honestly, I'm not there to entertain the children either. That doesn't mean I'll shy away from anything that can make the message as engaging as possible. I want the children to be excited about coming into the sanctuary and discovering new ways to experience and share God's amazing love. But an exciting presentation without a core message — that's entertainment.

Okay, it's confession time. There have been times when I felt there was either (a.) very little energy in the room or (b.) so much energy that I might, at any second, lose control of the room. And in those panicky moments I wasn't thinking "How can I get the message across to the children effectively?" I was thinking, "Please God, don't let me embarrass myself." So I went for the easy laugh. Everyone had a great time, but no one could really tell me what the children's moment was about.

What I hope I've learned is to not gauge the effectiveness of a children's moment based on the audience reaction (and here I'm using "audience" intentionally). Some of the best children's moments I've ever seen or been part of didn't end with a bang, but with a gentle "Amen."

On the Other Hand: I think there's a misconception among some that anything in worship that elicits laughter, cheers, or even applause is automatically considered "just entertainment." But there's no reason the children's moment can't be playful and meaningful at the same time. While it's important to not lose sight of the message, it's just as important to do what it takes to make that message stick! When we can effectively use music, games, movement, and laughter to teach children about God's love, these become more than tricks of the trade. They're tools of the trade.

Not Your Typical Sunday: No two Sundays are created equal. There are some days when the kids are simply going to be very active whether I want them to be or not. So I might as well make action, and lots of it, an integral part of that morning's children's moment. Here are a few Sundays when a more physically active children's moment is a really good idea:

- The Sunday after Thanksgiving — By the time I see the children on this morning they've either been out of school since Wednesday, or they got the entire week off. Just about every child's weekly routine has been disrupted in some way, and they don't know quite how to cope. If I try to do a sit-down, talky-talk children's moment, I'm going to lose their attention faster than you can say, "Pass the cranberry sauce." Get 'em up. Get 'em moving.

- Palm Sunday — "Okay kids, we're going to hand you these palm branches. We want you to wave them high in the air during the processional hymn. Then we want you to hold those branches very still so we can talk to you about churchy things like the literal meaning of the word *hosanna*." I don't think so. Make the waving of the palm branches central to the children's moment, because if you don't, the kids will.

- Easter Sunday — The majority of kids have already had chocolate before they even got dressed for church. Need I say more?

There are also a few Sundays when a gentler approach is best.

- The First Sunday of the New School Year — This is often the Sunday when many children give the children's moment a try for the first time (or when parents make their children give it a try). This isn't the Sunday to do something over the top. This is a day for building trust. Also, I like to remind parents that they are more than welcome to come down with their children. We want this to be a positive experience for the children, and if having Mom or Dad nearby helps, that's just fine.

- The Sunday after Christmas — This is always a light Sunday in terms of attendance. So I like to stay away from anything that might make the children feel more on the spot than they already do.

Where the People Are: Most of the time I base the children's moment on the primary Scripture and/or the theme of the senior minister's sermon. But there are certain Sundays when the children have many things on their minds, and church is not one of them (yet another great lesson from "The Ant and the Grasshopper" and Santa Claus). Halloween or Valentine's Day might be right around the corner. Even sacred times like Christmas and Easter have very powerful secular counterparts. Now, we can gear up with our "reason for the season" speeches while plowing ahead with whatever the sermon series or Common Lectionary suggests. But I choose to go a different way. Here's how I look at it — Jesus was, among other things, an outstanding teacher. He went where the people were, and used their everyday experiences as a springboard to teach important lessons about the nature of God's love. What a great role model!

So for example, on Easter Sunday when many children have visions of egg hunts and Easter bunnies dancing through their heads, what am I going to do? Am I going to tell the children to put those ideas out of their heads (already an uphill battle before the children's moment has even started) and require they focus on what Easter is all about? Or do I dare do the unthinkable and actually bring the Easter Bunny into the conversation…in church?! For me that decision is SO easy. Use their everyday experiences as a springboard to teach about God's love.

Etch-a-Sketch: One of the most frequent questions I get from others who lead children's moments is "What do you do when a child is determined to be a distraction during the children's moment?" Here's my little checklist:

1. If it's a minor distraction and not really affecting anyone else, let it go.

2. If it's a minor distraction and is affecting some of the other children, I simply walk over to where the distraction is coming from and make eye-contact with the child who is off-task.

3. If it's a major distraction — usually an enthusiastic child trying to tell me something about her week, often with a raised hand — I will either motion for the child to lower her hand, or ask the child to wait until the children's moment is over. She can tell me then, and I will be happy to hear all about it.

4. If it's a major distraction where the child's agenda clearly seems to be to draw attention to himself at the expense of all else, I will stop the children's moment. Then I will say to the child, as calmly as possible, "I would like for you to listen to me. I really believe that what I have to teach is very important, and I don't want you or your friends to miss a single word. Okay?" This is usually met with agreement. Make sure, if the child is able to stay even remotely focused, to offer positive reinforcement afterwards. "Thank you so much for paying attention. It means a lot to me that you tried your best."

5. Sometimes it takes more than a little self-control to keep my cool when a child is being willfully distracting. I don't want to shame or embarrass a child. Do you remember playing with an Etch-a-Sketch? I had one as a kid. You draw pictures on a rectangular screen using a couple of knobs. If the picture didn't turn out the way you wanted it to, no worries. You simply shook the Etch-a-Sketch, which gave you a clean slate to start anew. Now, I'm not suggesting you shake the children. I am suggesting that, when a children's moment goes into a tailspin…do the Etch-a-Sketch. You can say, "You know what? This isn't turning out how I'd like. Let's all stand up and do the Etch-a-Sketch." *(Invite the children to stand and lead them through the Etch-a-Sketch.)* "Let's shake our bodies head to toe. Shake, shake, shake! Shake, shake, shake! On the count of three, everybody freeze. One,

two, three, FREEZE! Now let's all have a seat, and try this whole children's moment again." This works great, but don't go to the Etch-a-Sketch too often. Save it for when you really need it.

6. Some children who can't seem to sit still or keep from speaking out are still truly doing the best they can. Other children may be fairly new to the church and a children's moment might be an unfamiliar experience for them. Still others spend time between two households with two sets of rules, expectations, and parenting styles. When all else fails, I take a deep breath and try to be as patient and gracious as possible. And since I've led children's moments on both patience and grace, I guess I've got to walk the walk, right?

The Bigger Picture: The concept of a children's moment has its critics. Some feel it's just parading the children up to the front for the entertainment of the adults. I can't disagree. I've seen this happen all too often.

Some feel it's mostly about reassuring the congregation that everything is okay, we still have some young families. No argument here either.

Some feel that a 5-minute children's moment gives tacit permission for the other 55 minutes of worship to fly completely over the heads of most children. "Shh! You got your time. Now it's time for the real worship to begin. Can't you just draw a picture in your bulletin or something?" Those of you who know me know that I am PASSIONATE about children and worship. Does a 7-year-old really need worship any less than a 57-year-old? I've encountered more than a few people who've actually answered "yes" to this.

True Story — We recently had an Easter service for children and families in an outdoor play area. Word had gotten out that we were going to release live butterflies. We had over 300 people show up. Three hundred children and their families PLUS live butterflies can make for one boisterous service. (Actually, the butterflies were pretty quiet and reasonably well-behaved.) No sooner was the service over than I was confronted by an adult. He was very upset because our worship service had disturbed his Sunday school class. I apologized and tried to explain that the children had just had a wonderful service. His response, "But the children already have the children's moment. Isn't that enough?" Wow! He just came right out and said it.

That sentiment is out there. Usually it's more cleverly concealed. When I walk into a church to attend a worship service, it isn't uncommon for me to see something in the bulletin or on the screen to the effect of — "Welcome to Fill-in-the-Blank Church. We are so glad you are here. We want you to know that we have a wonderful children's wing with great age-appropriate activities for your child while you attend worship." That all looks and sounds reasonable enough, but it's code for — "This worship service is really for adults. Your child would find it boring, and may even become a distraction to some of our other adult worshipers. Please take your child to the children's wing. Maybe they'll sing the Zacchaeus song. Maybe they'll make macaroni necklaces. We don't know for sure. What we do know is that with them out of the way, we'll be able to do real, adult-centered worship." I could go on, but you get the idea.

To those who would shy away from providing a weekly children's moment based on some of the above critiques I would simply say, let's not get too carried away here. Is it perfect? No. Is anything? But if we wait until all the lights are green before we step on the gas, we're never going to get anywhere. If we are serious about including children in worship in a meaningful way, a children's moment can be a step in the right direction.

On the other hand, for those of us who provide a weekly children's moment, but nothing else of real substance for children in worship, our work isn't done. A children's moment is a good start, but it can be more. It can be a catalyst for real change in the way a congregation views children and worship.

Let's Do Something

THEME

We don't go to church just to hear inspiring words. God's people are people of action.

SCRIPTURE

James 1:22 — Be doers of the word, not merely hearers.

In the Moment

It's important to get plenty of exercise. Let's all go to the gym. (*Invite the children to stand with you and pretend you are walking to the gym. Then have them pantomime with you as you narrate.*)

Okay, here we are at the gym. Let's put on our sneakers. Now let's put on our head bands, so no sweat gets in our eyes. Next, we need to stretch so we don't pull a muscle. Let's all reach way up high. Now let's reach down and touch our toes. All right, that ought to do it. (*Sit down. Most will sit down with you, though some will be confused. Explain.*)

Oh, we're not actually going to work out. But hey, we've got on the right clothes, and we're in the gym, so we should get in shape in no time, right? (*Some kids will say, "Wrong!"*)

Hmm, this isn't going so well. I don't feel any more in shape. Well, let's skip it for now because I have a better idea — let's all be in an orchestra. (*Have the children pantomime with you again as you narrate.*)

First, let's grab our violins and head for Symphony Hall. (*Pretend to walk to Symphony Hall. Once you get there, look around as if in awe.*)

Wow! Symphony Hall! What an amazing place! And here we are. Let's all get out our violins. Now we need to tune them. Finally, we need to make sure we have the right sheet music on our stands. All right, that ought to do it. (*Sit down and place your hands in your lap. Once again, most of the kids will sit with you. Some may try to play their pretend violins.*)

Oh, we aren't actually going to play any music. But hey, we're here in Symphony Hall, and we've got our violins and our sheet music. So it's just as exciting as playing in a great orchestra, right? (*More protests from the kids.*)

Okay, let's try this one more time. Let's all go to worship. *(One more time have the children pantomime with you as you narrate.)*

First we need to get dressed for church. Let's all put on our church clothes. *(I'll leave it at that. Each church and family has its own interpretation of what "church clothes" means.)* Now let's walk into the sanctuary. Ooh, it's so pretty in here. Now let's all find a seat and listen to some inspiring words. *(Once again, just sit there. Sit silently for almost an uncomfortably long period. When you start to get looks from the kids who are thinking, "Well?! Now what?!" continue.)*

Oh, we're not actually going to do anything. We're just going to listen to the words of God and then go about our business. That's good enough right? *(Perhaps some protests.)* But we're here in church. And we're wearing our church clothes. That's all there is to it, right? Right?! *(Hopefully by now all the kids are protesting, perhaps even loudly.)*

You know, I think you're right. We need to do more than just listen to the inspiring words of God. We need to DO what God wants us to do. If we want to get some exercise, we've got to do more than just put on the right clothes and show up at the gym. We've got to get up and get moving. Let's do ten jumping jacks. Here we go. *(Lead the children in doing ten jumping jacks.)*

If we want to play in a great orchestra, we've got to do more than just show up at Symphony Hall and sit with our violins in our laps. We've got to play those instruments. Let's play our violins. *(Lead the children in playing their pretend violins, perhaps to the tune of "Ode to Joy.")*

Let's be true followers of God, by doing more than just sitting and listening to inspiring words. Let's do what God's words say we should do.

CLOSING
Have the children march in place and repeat after you each line of the following prayer.

I will use my feet.
I will use my hands.
I will help God's people,
And do all that I can.
Amen. Amen.
Amen. Amen. Amen.

THe WØRLD NeeDS YØU tØ Be YØU

THeMe
You don't need to be like everyone else. Be your best you.

SCRiPTURe
1 Corinthians 12:14-20 — Many parts, but one body

PRePaRe
For this children's moment you need to coordinate with three helpers who can play very simple rhythms using body percussion or rhythm instruments. You might consider asking a few members of the adult choir to help you. Most of them would welcome the chance to do something more light-hearted than, say, "Surely He Hath Borne Our Griefs" or "Nothing But the Blood." If you use rhythm instruments, each of the four of you will need: a small frame drum, a rattle, a pair of sticks, and a pair of finger cymbals. You will also need to set aside a few minutes to run through this children's moment with your volunteer percussionists. And feel free to adapt this to your comfort level. You can have only three total percussionists, or several. You can use store-bought percussion instruments or ones made from recycled materials and other found objects.

In THe MØMent
Hi there. As you can see, I brought some friends with me today. We wanted to play a percussion jam for you. Here we go.

You and the three volunteers pick up the frame drums and play a simple, sparse rhythm in unison. Repeat the simple rhythm several times then stop.

Well, that didn't sound quite the way I'd hoped. (*To the volunteers*) What if we all play the rattles? Maybe that'll do it.

You and the volunteers put down the frame drums and pick up the rattles. All play a simple rhythm of steady beats over and over, and after several seconds, stop this as well.

That wasn't any better than the first time. In fact, it was pretty boring. Let's all play the sticks this time.

Put down the rattles and pick up the sticks. Play these on the off-beats (2 and 4) for several seconds then stop.

This isn't getting any better. We're all playing the same thing, on the same instruments, but it's all kind of, well, "blah." I know, let's all play the finger cymbals together. Nothing brings excitement to a percussion jam like finger cymbals.

Put down the sticks and pick up the finger cymbals. All play one time and let the cymbals ring. When the last sounds have completely died down, look around bewildered.

You know, we've tried everything. We tried it with all of us playing the same thing on the drums, on the rattles, on the sticks, on the finger cymbals, but... Hey! Wait just a second! *(as if making some bold discovery)* What if each of us plays a different instrument, and a different rhythm on that instrument, and we put all those different sounds… together? Let's give it a try.

Start by playing the simple rhythm on the drum. Keep repeating the simple rhythm and then add a volunteer playing the rattle with a steady beat. Several seconds later, add a volunteer playing the sticks on the off-beats. You can have the three of you get louder and softer, whatever you're comfortable doing. Then at the very end, stop and have a volunteer play the finger cymbals as a punctuator.

Wow! Now that's more like it! When we all tried to do the same thing and sound the same, the jam was boring. But when each of us added something special that none of the others was doing, it made the percussion jam exciting and fun. Different sure is good. Thanks to God for making all of us different, and for making all of us with something special to bring.

CLOSING

Let's close by having one more big percussion jam. And we want you to join us. Pick your favorite body percussion sound — stomping, patting, clapping, snapping, tongue clicks, beat-boxing, you name it — and join us as we play.

Play the same rhythms as before. The kids might play the same rhythms you and the volunteers are playing. They may go in a completely different direction. Either way is just fine. It doesn't have to be a Grammy-winning performance.

Answering the Call

THEME
We can answer Jesus' call to love God by helping others.

SCRIPTURE
John 10:1-4 — The Voice of the Shepherd

PREPARE
Gather four animal puppets or stuffed animals. Before worship enlist the help of four volunteers who can sit in different areas of the worship space, each with one of the puppets. Make sure the volunteers keep their animal puppets hidden. When an animal is "called" during the children's moment, the volunteer with the corresponding puppet will make that puppet pop up so it can be seen by all the children.

In the Moment
Did you know that we have animals right here in the sanctuary? Well, we do. But they won't come out unless we call them. I think there might be a sheep in here somewhere. How would we call a sheep? *(Several children will start to baa.)* That's right. Let's all call the sheep. Baa. *(Have the children baa with you. When the sheep pops up many children will point "There it is! There it is!")* Yep. There's the sheep.

I wonder if there's a rooster in here. How would we call a rooster? *(Children will cock-a-doodle-doo.)* Let's all call the rooster. *(Have the children cock-a-doodle-doo with you until the rooster pops up.)* There's the rooster.

I wonder what other animals are in here. Let's try calling a cow. *(Have the children moo with you. Once again, when the cow pops up, the children will all point it out.)* There's the cow. Wow! There sure are a lot of animals in here.

I wonder if there's a wolf in here. Let's try calling a wolf. *(Have the children howl with you until the wolf pops up. By the way, if you use a wolf puppet, have this volunteer sit further back. A wolf puppet, no matter how soft and cute, is still a wolf to some children.)* There's the wolf, way back there.

Before we go on, let me ask some questions. Who here would help up your friend if she fell down? *(Most children will raise their hands.)*

Who would share a meal with someone if they forgot their lunch? *(Most will raise their hands.)* Who would pray for a family member who was sick? *(Again, most will raise their hands.)*

Guess what? You all just answered a call, too. *(You might get some puzzled expressions.)* Well, we didn't hear anyone saying, "Hello! Kids?! Yodel-lay-hee-hoo!" *(giggles)* But you heard three questions about helping other people and said that, yes, you would help. That means you are willing to do what Jesus calls us to do. That's wonderful.

Closing
Invite the children to repeat after you each line of the following prayer.

I may be young.
I may be small.
But I will answer
Jesus' call.
Amen.

WONDERFULLY MADE

THEME
We are wonderfully made by God, and we were made for change.

SCRIPTURE
Psalm 139:13-14 — I am fearfully and wonderfully made. See also Revelation 21:5 — I am making all things new.

In the Moment
God made a wonderful world full of amazing animals, plants, trees, rivers, mountains, and so much more. One of the things that makes God's creation so amazing is that God made it for change.

Let's celebrate one of God's creatures that goes through a lot of changes in a very short time. Let's be frogs. *(Some kids will start hopping and croaking right away.)* But first we have to start as frog eggs, so let's all roll up into balls as small as we can get.

Lead the children to join you in all of the actions as you narrate what to do.

So now we are all frog eggs. We're just hanging out in the water, waiting to hatch. We are wonderfully made by God who loves us very much.

Now we need to hatch out of these eggs, but we won't become full-grown frogs yet. First we must become tadpoles. Ready? Here we go. *(Have the children join you in hatching out of the eggs and being tadpoles by putting a hand behind you to swish like a tail.)*

Wow! That was a pretty big change. We've gone from eggs to tadpoles. We are still wonderfully made, and God still loves us very much. Let's swim around in the water with our swishy tails. *(Invite the children to swim with you.)*

Now we have to go through more changes. It's time to grow four good, strong legs. *(Have the children join you in stretching out arms and legs.)*

Hey, look at our webbed toes. That will be helpful for swimming around in the water, especially since our tails are almost gone. And now it's time to make one more big change. It's time for us to climb out of the water and start hopping around with these legs. Ready? Here we go. *(Lead the children through the steps of climbing out of the imaginary water and hopping in place. Start making a buzzing sound.)*

Hey, there's a fly. I don't know about you, but I'm one hungry frog. I could sure go for a snack. Let's use our long sticky tongues to catch flies. *(Have the children join you in pretending to snatch flies right out of the air. Some will pretend to be grossed out by this, but mostly they'll have fun.)*

Mm, mm good! You know, we frogs went through a lot of changes, and all along the way we were wonderfully made and God loved us very much.

God's creation is full of changes. Frogs change, seasons change, and people just like us — we change too. It's important to remember every step of the way that we are wonderfully made and God loves us very much.

CLOSING
Have the children repeat after you each line of the following prayer poem.

From acorn to oak tree,
From tadpole to frog,
From raindrop to river,
From puppy to dog:
God made us all special,
But one thing we know,
We've all got to change
In order to grow.
Amen.

BY THE WAY
We could've done the caterpillar/cocoon/butterfly thing, but that's been done so many times. Frogs deserve their moment, too!

THERE IS ONLY US

THEME
There is no "us and them," only us.

SCRIPTURE
Luke 10:25-37–The Good Samaritan — Who is my neighbor?

PREPARE
This one takes a fair amount of prep-work, but the results are worth it! In a box place the following items: a small model of a church or a photo of your own church, a cut-out of the state where you live (I got ours from a wooden 50 states puzzle), a small U.S. flag, and a small inflatable globe which is not currently inflated. Now, the over-the-top part is this — prior to worship — enlist the help of eight volunteers to sit out in different areas of the worship space, each with one of the other eight planets (Earth is in the box). Yes, I said "the other eight planets." I still include Pluto. What can I say? I have a hard time letting some things go.

Instruct the eight volunteers to keep the planets hidden until their portion near the end of the children's moment when you have the children blow three times.

In the Moment
You see I have a box with me. But before we look inside the box, let's look out at the grownups in the congregation. There they are out there. And here we are up here. It's us and them. But hold on a second. Let's zoom out a little bit. Everyone zoom out with me.

Each time you zoom out, have the kids join you in pretending to turn an imaginary crank several times and make a whirring sound. Reach into the box and bring out the little model church.

What is this? *(The children will say "A church.")* That's right, it's a church. Let's imagine it's our church. See? We're all in here together. There's not really us and them. There's just us. Then again, there are those outside this church. So maybe it's us here in the church, and everyone outside the church is them.

It's time to zoom out again. *(Zoom out, and bring the cut-out of your state out of the box.)* What state is this? *(You may want to write the name of your state on the shape, just to help. Our kids, of course, said Texas.)*

That's right. It's the state of Texas. And everyone in the state, inside or outside this church, is a Texan. So it's not really us and them. It's just us. Then again, there are those who live outside the state, you know, like in Oklahoma, Arkansas, even Idaho! So maybe it's us here in Texas, and everyone outside the state is them.

Let's zoom out some more. *(Zoom out, and bring the little U.S. flag out of the box.)* What flag is this? *(Children will answer "America" or "United States.")* Yes. It's the United States flag. And everyone in the United States, from Texas to Idaho is part of the same country. So it's not really us and them. It's just us. Then again, there are those who live outside the United States, in other countries like Honduras or Uzbekistan. So maybe it's us here in the United States, and everyone outside the country is them.

It's time to zoom out again. *(Zoom out, bring the inflatable globe out of the box and inflate it.)* Okay, what have we here? *(Children will say "The World" or "Earth.")* Right! It's the earth. And everyone on earth, from here to Uzbekistan is part of the same world. So it's not really us and them. It's just us. Then again, what if there are…others? Maybe earth isn't the only place where someone could live.

We need to zoom out one more time, but I'm afraid if I had to do all the inflating for this next one, I'd get lightheaded. So I need your help. Let's blow three times. Here we go! *(Lead the children as you all blow three times. On the third blow, have the eight volunteers with the other planets stand wherever they are in the worship space. The kids, and the rest of the congregation, will really like this.)*

Wow! Look, it's the whole solar system. All the planets are here, even Pluto. No matter how many times we think there's an us and a them, all we have to do is zoom out and see that it's all just us. Jesus spent a lot of his time trying to teach anyone who would listen, that it's all just us.

CLOSING
After you recite each line, invite the children to respond simply with the word "us."

Everyone in our church,
Us.
Everyone in our state,
Us.
Everyone in our country,
Us.

Everyone in the world.
Us.
There is no us and them. There is only…
Us.

D⎁⎁RS

THEME

We need to take all that we learn in church through the doors and out into the world.

SCRIPTURE

Revelation 3:8 — I have put an open door before you. See also Colossians 4:3.

PREPARE

Use four pieces of foam core to make four different doors. (You may use poster board or, if you have a smaller worship space, four pieces of cardstock.) Each door is to represent a different store or building.

Door 1 – a door to a school. You can decorate this door by using markers to draw numbers, letters of the alphabet, an apple.

Door 2 – a door to a doctor's office. This door can be decorated with pictures of bandages and a stethoscope.

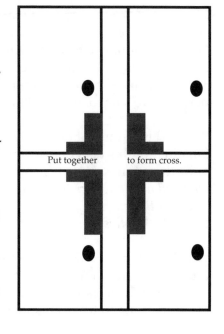

Put together   to form cross.

Door 3 – a door to a hardware store. You can decorate this door with pictures of tools, such as a hammer, screwdriver, and a saw.

Door 4 – a door to a grocery store. This door can be decorated with pictures of bread, cheese, fruits, and vegetables.

All four doors can have pictures of doorknobs on the far right side, about halfway up.

Also, each door needs to have a portion of a cross in one of the corners, so that when all four doors are put together — two on top and two below — the picture of the cross can be seen.

Have four volunteers planted throughout the worship space, each with a door. Have the volunteers keep their doors hidden until the appropriate times. Make sure each volunteer knows the order of the doors, 1 through 4.

In the Moment

Knock, knock.
(Kids say, "Who's there?")
Thistle.
(Kids say, "Thistle who?")
Thistle be a message about doors.
(Kids laugh hysterically despite the fact the joke is a true "groaner.")

There are a lot of doors. Let's take a look at some and see if we can guess what would be on the other side. Where is Door 1? *(The volunteer with Door 1 holds it up for the kids to see. Go over to the door and look at it.)* This door has numbers and letters of the alphabet. Where does it lead? *(The kids will say, hopefully, "To school. It's a school!")* Right, it's a door to a school. If we go inside we can learn so much, like how to read, how to multiply, how to spell Timbuktu. But if we learn all those cool things and never walk back through that door into the world, all the learning in the world won't do any good.

Let's see if we can spot Door 2. *(The volunteer with Door 2 holds it up for the kids to see. Run over to it.)* This door has bandages and a stethoscope. Where would you find this door? *(Kids will answer, "At the doctor.")* Yes, it's a door to a doctor's office. Whenever we feel sick or hurt, we can walk through this door and see a doctor who can help us feel better. But once we get what we need to help us feel better, if we don't go back through the door and into the world, feeling better won't matter all that much.

Where's Door 3? *(The volunteer with Door 3 holds it up for the kids to see. Go over to it.)* Where do you suppose this door leads? *(The kids, seeing the tools may say it goes to a hardware store, a tool shed, or even a construction site.)* This would make a great door for a hardware store. When we walk through the door we can get all kinds of tools we need for building and fixing things. But once we get the tools, if we don't go back through the door and into the world, we won't be able to build or fix anything.

Now let's look for Door 4. *(The volunteer with Door 4 holds it up for the kids to see. Go to it.)* Where would this door go? *(Kids will say a grocery store or supermarket.)* It's a grocery store door. When we walk through this door we can get all kinds of wonderful things to eat — cheese, bread, apricots, Brussels sprouts, zucchini. But once we get this great food, if we don't go back through the door and into the world, we can't cook it or put it in a salad.

There's one more door. Let's see what happens if we put all four of these doors together. *(Have the four volunteers come forward and hold their respective doors together in such a way that it looks like one really big door with a large cross in the center.)*

If we walked through this door, where would we be? *(The kids will say, "Church.")* Yes, it's a church door. When we go inside we can learn amazing things; we can find ways to feel better; we can also learn things to help us build and things that feed us. But if we don't go back through the door and into the world, none of it will do us, or the world, much good.

It's up to us to take all the wonderful things we learn and experience here in church and share it all with the world.

And the door to God's church has something special that no other door has — two entrances. There is no exit — only an entrance into the building, and an entrance into the world.

CLOSING
Knock, knock.
(Kids say, "Who's there?")
Lettuce.
(Kids say, "Lettuce who?")
Lettuce pray.

Offer this prayer on behalf of all those present.

Gracious God.
There are so many doors.
Help us remember that the door of your church
Is a door into our hearts
And a door into the world.
There are no exits to your love.
Amen.

THAT EXTRA WOW FACTOR
At the moment when you say "The door of the church is an entrance into the world," have the four volunteers turn their doors around to reveal a big picture of the world on the other side. This is very effective and isn't that hard to pull off. Remember that in order to make the picture of the world in the center when it's turned to face the kids, the four pieces of the world must be drawn on the outer edges of the backs on the four doors.

Nana's Visit

THEME
Some people in our lives seem to be there just to make us try harder and be better. Thank God we have these people in our lives.

SCRIPTURE
1 Samuel 10:6-7 — Go and do what your hand finds to do.

PREPARE
Collect the following props: a stuffed animal, a sweater, a plastic cup and plate, several leaves (or leaves cut out of paper), and a plastic bin to hold everything.

In the Moment
As the children come down for their time with you, toss the stuffed animal and sweater to one spot on the floor. Next to that place the plastic cup and plate. And next to that scatter the leaves.

It was Saturday morning and I couldn't wait to get on my bike and ride around the neighborhood all day. I had my helmet on and my hand on the doorknob when my mom called out, "Mark. Did you forget? Nana is coming in today and she's staying in your room. You have to clean your room before you can do anything else." *(sigh)* So I took off my helmet, walked back to my room, and started to straighten things up.

(As you say the next part, slowly fold the sweater, and place it carefully in the plastic bin. Put the stuffed animal on top.) It seemed like it took forever. And all the time I kept waiting for a sign that Nana had come. Whenever she came over, she always knocked her special knock. *(Demonstrate a special knock. I used the rhythm to Shave and a Haircut.)*

The sooner she got there, the sooner I could stop cleaning. I listened…but I didn't hear the knock. Finally, after a million minutes, I walked out of my clean room when my mom said it was time for lunch. "Great!" I thought. "After lunch I'll still have all afternoon to ride my bike."

But after lunch Mom said, "You know, Mark, while you're in the kitchen, you might as well wash the dishes and put them away." *(sigh)* *(Take the cup and plate and slowly put them in the bin.)* So I put away the dishes, still listening for that knock. *(Demonstrate the special knock again.)* But…nothing. Still no Nana. Finally I got the dishes all put away and was headed outside when Mom said, "Mark, if you're going outside, will you rake the leaves?"

"But Mom," I protested, "I've been working all day, and I really wanted to ride my bike, and soon it's going to be getting too late, and my whole Saturday will be ruined!"

Mom responded, "But Mark, don't you want everything to look nice for when your Nana gets here?"

"Yes, ma'am." *(sigh)* So I went outside to pick up leaves. *(Slowly gather the leaves and place them in the plastic bin.)* It took as long to clean the outside of the house as it did to clean the inside of the house. I was feeling like life was pretty unfair. I even thought it would've been better if Nana wasn't coming at all. At least then I would've been able to ride my bike. But then I saw how great the yard looked, and I didn't feel too bad.

And then I walked back into the house through the kitchen. The kitchen looked pretty nice, and I knew I had been a part of that. I went and looked at my bedroom. The whole house looked great. If Nana wasn't coming, none of it would have looked like that. Sure I missed out on riding my bike, but I had to admit, seeing everything I had accomplished that day made me feel pretty good. And then I heard the knock at the door…*(Demonstrate the special knock.)*…and I felt even better.

CLosing
Offer this prayer on behalf of all present.

Loving God,
Sometimes I think you put people in our lives just to make us work.
Sometimes I think you put people in our lives just to make us try harder,
Or to do better.
Well, thanks for doing that. It works.
Amen.

Okay, I eMBeLLiSHeD a Bit
My Nana doesn't really have a special knock. Here's what she does — every time she pulls into her driveway at home (or the familiar driveway of a family member she's visiting) she always says the same thing, "Home again, home again! Piggity, pig!" It's one of the many things I love about my Nana. But it's hard to hear that from inside the house, so I "played" with the details a bit. Just so you know.

CHANGE

THEME
Change is a part of life. Rather than trying to stop change altogether, we can help shape it in positive ways.

SCRIPTURE
Genesis 12; 17; 18; and 21 — Abraham and Sarah

PREPARE
You will need to gather a few materials:
- *a large plastic bin that is completely opaque*
- *a watering can with water*
- *two potted flowers, such as gerbera daisies*
- *a bucket that can be turned upside down and placed inside the plastic bin*
- *a funnel*
- *three lengths of ½-inch PVC pipe (one 12-inch length, and two 6-inch lengths)*
- *two ½-inch PVC elbow joints (90 degrees)*

That all seems like a lot. Don't worry! This is really a straightforward children's moment, and you can get most of these items in one trip to a hardware store.

Before worship you will need to set up a table on which to set the plastic bin.
1. *Place one potted flower inside the bin on the bottom so that it cannot be seen at all.*
2. *Place the bucket upside down in the bin next to the potted flower on the bottom.*
3. *Next, place the other potted flower on top of the overturned bucket so that it can be easily seen.*
4. *Place the PVC pipes, elbow joints, and the funnel inside the large plastic bin. These items will be assembled during the children's moment to create a kind of rain gutter.*
5. *Recruit a volunteer to hold the watering can.*

There! That's the set-up. Now comes the easy part.

IN THE MOMENT
Change is an important part of life. And change can be refreshing, like a gentle rain after many very, very dry days.

At this point, have the volunteer with the watering can start to gently water the flower that is showing out of the bin. You don't really acknowledge the watering process in words. It's more there to be a powerful visual to reinforce what you're talking about.

Change can make a difference. Change can help things grow.

Watch as the water pours onto the flower for a few seconds. But the watering does not stop and might even start to overflow the flower pot. Now you see why a big plastic bin is so helpful.

Change can be a good thing. Then again, there can also be too much of a good thing. When we see change threaten to damage something we've spent time and energy growing, it makes us want to stop that change.

Cup hands under the watering can and try to catch the water so it doesn't reach the flower.

We can hold the change back for a while, but eventually…(*The water will start to trickle over and through your fingers and onto the flower. Accentuate this a bit.*)…change happens anyway, and we end up making a big mess.

Show your dripping wet hands. By the way, did I mention this is a very WET children's moment? Begin assembling the rain gutter using the PVC pipes, elbow joints, and funnel. Start by holding the 12-inch length of pipe parallel with the ground. Attach an elbow joint to each end of the pipe, the end closest to the watering can facing up, and the end closest to the hidden flower facing down. Attach a 6-inch length of pipe to each elbow joint. You should now have what looks like a letter Z on its side. Place the funnel in the top of the length of pipe which is facing up. It should be the one nearest the watering can. Now, that took a while to type, but should take mere seconds to actually put together.

Rather that simply going along with change for the sake of change, or resisting any change no matter what, there is another option. What if we get in front of that change, and help shape it?

Place the funnel directly under the spout of the watering can. The water should trickle through the pipes and onto the hidden flower.

If we help shape the change, who knows? Not only might we preserve those things we've spent so much time caring for, but… (*Reach into the bin and bring out the flower that was hidden and is now receiving water.*)…maybe we can even help something new to grow as well. (*After a few seconds the volunteer can stop watering.*)

CLOSING
Invite the children to repeat after you each line of the following poem prayer.

Some changes are easy.
Some changes are tough.
Some changes convince us
That we've had enough.
From season to season,
From night into day
God's love will be with us
Each step of the way.
Amen.

LAYERS OF MEANING
A typical children's moment at our church has children ranging in age from 2 to 11. So I believe in teaching to that range, rather than always trying to hit an average age. That means sometimes the children's moment is going to be geared slightly toward the older children. This is one of those children's moments. The older children will like to make the connections between the watering of the flowers and changes going on in their own lives. The younger children will experience the watering of the flowers and the words about change as two distinct things. And that's okay, as long as I don't lean too heavily on "like" and "as" to get through. Actually, I only use the word "like" one time, when comparing change to rain. Otherwise each element, the verbal and the visual, may be taken at face value, synthesized into one by those ready for that level of thought.

GOOD IS WHAT WE DO

THEME
We help others know about God's love by showing that love, not simply talking about it.

SCRIPTURE
Matthew 28:16-20 — As you go, make disciples.

PREPARE
Make a bracelet out of duct tape. Use a black marker to write the first letters in the phrase "What Would A Kid At (name of your church) Do?" In the case of our church, my bracelet read WWAKAFUMCD (What Would A Kid At First United Methodist Church Do?)

In the Moment
When worship is over, we'll go back through the doors of our church building and out into the world. We'll have many chances to share the wonder of God's love with others.

We can tell people about God's love. Maybe they'll listen. Maybe they won't. But we're First Methodist Kids *(use your church name throughout).* We can show people what God's love looks like by the things we do, and we won't even have to say a single word.

I'm wearing a bracelet to help remind me of something very important — What would a kid at First United Methodist Church Do? Or WWAKAFUMCD for short.

Let's try out a few things. Since it's still Sunday morning, and we're still in the sanctuary, we're going to have to fast-forward to tomorrow morning. The fast-forward button is behind your right ear. Let's press it and go to tomorrow morning. *(Invite the children to join in pressing their imaginary fast-forward buttons. You can even make whirring fast-forward sounds.)*

For the next several scenarios, pantomime the actions, and have the kids join in whenever possible so they aren't just sitting and listening.

Okay, it's Monday morning and here we are at school. We're sitting on the floor during story time when…look. A new kid walks in. She's a new student at school and she needs a place to sit down, but can't find a place. What would a First Methodist Kid do? *(Hopefully, the children will respond, "Share a place." or "Scoot over and make room.")*

We can make room. Let's scoot over and make room for our new classmate. Scoot, scoot, scoot. Scoot, scoot, scoot.

Okay, First Methodist Kids, let's fast-forward again. *(Have the kids press their fast-forward buttons.)*

It's now lunchtime. We're in the cafeteria eating our favorite lunch. We look over and see that one of our friends is very sad. He had spaghetti with tomato sauce and now he's got sauce all over his face, and even on his shirt. He's out of napkins, and we have an extra one. What would a First Methodist Kid do? *(The kids will say, "Share your napkin.")* That's a good idea. Let's share our napkin.

It's time to fast-forward again. *(Have the kids press their fast-forward buttons.)*

Now we're at afternoon recess, and we've been playing soccer. A player from the other team fell and scraped his knee. Everyone else has run after the ball, but you see that the player who fell hasn't gotten back up yet. What would a First Methodist Kid do? *(The kids will say, "Help him up," or "See if he is okay.")* Are you sure? He is on the other team, remember? *(The kids insist.)* You know, I think you're right. Let's go see if he's okay, and then help him up.

You know, you First Methodist Kids are amazing! You did some very kind things and helped many people. You showed people what God's love is all about.

CLOSING
There's something else First Methodist Kids can do — pray. Repeat after me:

Dear God,
Help us do good in the world.
We're First Methodist Kids,
And good is what we do.
Amen.

Opposite Day

THEME
Jesus came and turned everything upside down, lifting up the last and the least among us.

SCRIPTURE
Luke 9:48 — The least will be the greatest.

In the Moment
Good bye, grownups. *(confused looks from the kids)* Oops. I forgot to tell you — today is Opposite Day. So what ever I say means the opposite. When I say "good bye" I mean…*(The kids answer, "Hello.")* When I say "grownups" you know I really mean…*(The kids answer, "Kids.")*

You know, when Jesus came he made every day like Opposite Day. He taught that through God's love: The last will be…*(Allow the kids to respond "first.")* The poor will be…*("rich.")* And those who want to enter the kingdom of God must do so, not as grownups, but as…*("kids.")*

Okay, let's play the Opposite Game. Whatever I tell you to do, make sure to do the opposite. I'll indicate for the game to start by tapping my nose. And I'll tap my nose again to indicate when the game is over. Otherwise, at the end, I could tell you what a wonderful job you did, and you might think I meant the opposite. Here we go.

(Tap your nose to indicate the Opposite Game has begun.) Everyone sit down. *(Wait for them to stand up. It'll take a few rounds for the younger children to catch on.)* Make a sad face. *(The children make a happy face.)* Put your hands way down low. *(The children raise them high in the air.)* Hold them very still. *(The children wiggle their hands.)* Stand up. *(The children sit down. Tap your nose to indicate the game is over.)* You really did a great job!

CLOSING
Pray this short prayer on behalf of all present.

Dear God, Help us celebrate Opposite Day every day. When we would rather put ourselves first, help us put others first. When we would rather do all the talking, help us be good listeners. When we would rather get, help us to give. Amen.

Witnesses

THEME

We can use our eyes and ears to witness examples of God's amazing love. Others can witness us being examples of God's amazing love.

SCRIPTURE

Acts 1:1-8 — You will be my witnesses.

PREPARE

Make a card out of construction paper that says, "Have a great day." Collect a notepad and a pencil. An optional item is a bobby hat (think Keystone Cops). Recruit a volunteer to deliver the handmade card to a designated grownup in the congregation. Make sure the grownup in the congregation is willing to receive the card. No matter how brief the role seems to be, I never include an adult in a children's moment without asking. So far, I have yet to be told "no." It's amazing what our adults will do for our kids.

In the Moment

After inviting the children to come forward, stand to the side, preferably out of sight. Have the volunteer with the card enter and hand the card to the grownup in the congregation. The volunteer can smile, say, "It's so good to see you today," then walk off in the opposite direction from where you enter.

You enter holding the notepad and pencil and wearing the bobby hat if you have one. You look around for someone who seems to have just gotten away. Then you turn to the children.

Did you see someone just come through here? *(The children respond, "Yes!" and may even try to show you where that person went.)* It appears I have some witnesses. Did you happen to see what this person did? *(The children say something to the effect of, "He gave that lady a card and then ran away.")*

Where did you say this lady was? *(The children point to the person, who was in our case, a lady. Walk over to her.)*

Excuse me ma'am, did someone come through here and give you a card? *(She answers, "Yes," perhaps more shyly than the kids answer questions.)* Would you mind reading the card aloud, please? *(She opens the card and reads it aloud – Have a great day!)*

Aha! It's just as I suspected, we are on the scene of…an act of kindness! You are all witnesses who used your eyes to see someone do something very kind, and then you told me all about it. Now, I need to ask another question. Did this kind person say anything? *(The children may answer, "He said – It's good to see you." They may not get it exactly, but it should be close.)* Aha! Well that confirms it. This is the scene of an act of kindness.

As witnesses, you used your ears to listen as someone did something very kind, and then you told me about it. When we do kind things for others, it's a way we can show God's love. God would be very happy with this act of kindness. Did the person ever say anything about God? *(Most of the children will answer, "No." Then again, remember, you never know what the kids are going to say.)*

Even though the person never mentioned God by name, we were still able to witness God's love at work through an act of kindness. Let's all remember to keep our eyes and ears open. We can find many ways, day after day, to witness God's love in the world. And when we do kind things in the world, others can witness God's love in us!

CloSinG
Invite the children to repeat after you each line of the following poem prayer.

Guide me, Lord, in what I say.
Guide me in what I do,
That all the world may see your love,
And see that I love you.
Amen.

A TRicKY WoRD
Witness is not an easy word for kids; and I know plenty of adults who struggle with it, too. Children who have experience with the word mostly associate a witness with someone who observes a crime. So my first task was to provide an opportunity for the kids to associate *witness* with something positive — observing an act of kindness. The other big hurdle, and the one that trips many of us up, is when we are called to be witnesses of God's love. Perhaps some of us have had an uncomfortable experience in our past when a well-intentioned (or in some cases, not-so-well-intentioned) person tried to "save" us by witnessing. Maybe that's left us a little squeamish about being witnesses because we don't want to make others feel that same discomfort we felt. So my second task was to demonstrate that witnessing can be about so much more than what we say to others about God's love. It can be how we show God's love in action.

THINGS THAT JUST HAPPEN

THEME
There are so many things we think "just happen." But someone, often Mom or a mother figure, makes those things happen.

SCRIPTURE
Isaiah 66:13 — As a mother comforts her child

PREPARE
Using index cards (or card stock) and a marker make cards that read, What can I do for you? *Make enough cards for each child to receive one.*

In the Moment
Did you ever notice how some things just happen? Like when your school takes a field trip to the zoo, and you just happen to be able to get right on a bus and go to the zoo…or at suppertime a meal just happens to be there for us to eat…or it's very cold outside, but we wake up in the morning all warm and toasty because the covers just happen to be pulled up to our chin.

Guess what? Those things don't just happen. Someone makes those things happen. It could be a father, a grandparent, an aunt, an uncle, even an older brother or sister. Very often, the person who makes these things happen is…*(You can leave just the slightest pause here. The kids will most likely fill in the space you leave by saying, "Mothers!" or "Mom!")*

Moms do make things happen. And the reason we think the things they do "just happen" is because they do these things whether we ask or not. Think about it. The reason we get to go to the zoo is because someone made sure our permission slip was signed and that our health form was all filled out. By the way, those forms didn't "just happen" to end up in our backpacks on Monday morning so we could hand them to the teacher.

And we don't have to ask, "Mom? Is it okay if I eat some food today? I want to continue to grow and live 'n stuff. I think food might help." Maybe when we come home from school we can smell dinner being prepared. Maybe after a hard day at the office, Mom swings by and picks up Chinese food for everyone. And our favorite — Chicken lo Mein –

doesn't "just happen" to be there. Mom made sure it was there because she knows us and loves us.

And we sure don't say in our sleep, "Mom! I'm cold! Will you please pull the covers up for me." She knows we kick the covers off when we sleep, and because she loves us, she makes sure we're tucked in.

We're so lucky to have moms and mother figures in our lives. They really make things happen. And they make things happen in our lives because they love us. Let's do something to show our appreciation for their love.

Hand a card to each child.

Read your card and tell me what it says. (*The children will read, "What can I do for you?" Repeat this phrase couple of times so the pre-readers can feel included.*)

This is an important day to remember that we can do things for our wonderful moms and mother figures. Let's practice. Let's look out and find the eyes of our mothers, not just our moms, but all the wonderful women in our church who help bring us up in the faith. And all together let's ask them what's on your cards. Here we go. (*Lead the children in saying "What can I do for you?" If it's a little tentative, ask the children to repeat it.*)

I want each of you to give the card to your mom. You know why? People are all celebrating mothers today. But in a few weeks, your mom might really want to cash this card in. It's good to remember that every day we can help the people who make things happen in our lives.

CLOSING
Invite the children to repeat after you this brief prayer.

Loving God, thank you for mothers. Amen.

TO BE CLEAR
The two lines in this children's moment – "It could be a father, a grandparent, an aunt, an uncle, even an older brother or sister" and "Maybe after a hard day at the office, Mom swings by and picks up Chinese food for everyone" are not simply throw-away lines. They are vital. Our mothers are not merely servants for the rest of us. To celebrate mothers only for cooking and cleaning for us would be a little like me giving my wife a mop for her birthday. (I'm not that crazy.) And many of the roles traditionally associated with mothers can be, and often are, taken on by male figures in our lives. (I make a pretty mean Chicken Parmesan!)

Believe

Theme
Doubting and questioning do not mean you're a bad Christian. Jesus' closest friends struggled with what to believe in.

Scripture
John 20:19-29 — Jesus and Thomas

In the Moment
Today we're going to explore what it means to doubt. When we doubt, it means we're not sure just yet what we believe about something. It's okay to doubt. It's okay to question.

It doesn't make you a bad Christian to question things – even things you read in the Bible. In fact, it puts you in pretty good company. Jesus' closest friends and followers also had their doubts.

Invite the children to pantomime each of the following actions with you.

These were people who ate with Jesus,
Walked with Jesus,
And prayed with Jesus.

They knew he had died on a cross. And when he died they knew he was put in a tomb. On the third day some were saying Jesus had risen from the dead, that he was alive! But many of his closest friends had their doubts. One of those friends was Thomas.

Invite the children to pantomime each of the following actions with you.

Thomas had eaten with Jesus,
Walked with Jesus,
And prayed with Jesus.

But he wouldn't believe Jesus had risen until he could see Jesus with his own eyes and touch Jesus with his own hands.

One day Jesus did appear and let Thomas touch him. At once Thomas knew it was Jesus and that Jesus had risen. Jesus said that Thomas had seen and believed. He also said that blessed were those who hadn't even seen him at all, yet still believe. I think he was talking about us. Jesus' disciples were able to see him with their eyes and touch him with their hands. We are called to believe in Jesus because of what we read in the Bible and because of the love we feel for him in our hearts.

CLoSinG

While we don't have Jesus' actual in-the-flesh hands to touch, when we're having our doubts, we do have hands we can hold on to. I would like each of you to turn and take a neighbor's hand. *(There will be some squirming about this. Here are two things you can do. Invite the congregation to join in so the children don't feel like they're the only ones "having" to hold hands. And remind the children that holding hands in church for occasions like this is okay.)*

I want you to look at one another and say these words. *(Invite them to repeat after you.)*

When you have doubts,
I'm here for you.
When you feel alone,
I'm here for you.
When you want to celebrate,
I will laugh with you.
When you need to cry,
I will hold your hand.
If you believe in me,
And I believe in you,
Together we'll believe in this church,
Believe in Jesus,
And believe in the power of God's love.
Believe in that!
Amen.

ICK

A lot of congregations struggle with side-to-side things in worship like passing the peace or turning to a neighbor for a closing such as this one. Given enough opportunities, gently presented, many congregations truly embrace the experience. When we first started passing the peace in our own church, many people felt awkward and uncertain if it was "worshipful" enough. Now it's become a warm, smile-filled, and meaningful part of each service.

BUNNIES AND EGGS at CHURCH

THEME
Easter is a time to celebrate Jesus' life, teaching, and resurrection.

SCRIPTURE
Mark 16:1-8 — He is not here, but has risen.

PREPARE
Fill three plastic eggs, each with a different reminder note for you. Here is what the three notes should read:

1. *Don't forget about the ears.*
2. *Don't forget about the hopping thing.*
3. *Don't forget the basket.*

You will also need an Easter basket, a set of bunny ears for you to wear, and three willing adult volunteers to hold the plastic eggs in the worship space.

In the Moment
Today is Easter! It's a day when we celebrate that Jesus rose from the grave and will live in our hearts and our lives forever. What is something fun we do on Easter? *(It won't take long at all for the children to say, "Hunt Easter eggs!")* Well, let's have an Easter egg hunt right here, right now. Let's look out in the worship space and see if we can spot any Easter eggs.

This is the cue for the three adult helpers to hold up the plastic Easter eggs. The kids will go bonkers trying to show you where the eggs are. Very exciting! Go over to one of the eggs and bring it back to where the children are as you open it up and read the reminder note.

Here's an egg. Let's see if there's any chocolate inside. Hmm. No chocolate, just a note. It says, "Don't forget the ears." Ah yes, the ears. *(Put on the bunny ears.)* Do you know why I'm wearing these ears? *(The kids will say, "Because of the Easter Bunny.")* The Easter Bunny? I'm wearing these ears to remind us to keep our ears open to hear how Jesus is alive today. Put on your ears, too. *(Invite the children to use their hands to make big bunny ears.)*

Every time we hear a beautiful song sung by the choir or hear someone talk about how they are going to give their money or time to help others, we can know that Jesus lives. Let's see if we can find another egg.

The children will show you where to look. Go get the next egg and walk back to the children as you open it and read the reminder note.

Here's another egg. There's no chocolate in this one either. There's a note. It says, "Don't forget the hopping thing." Right, the hopping thing. (*Start hopping.*) Do you know why I'm hopping? (*The children will insist, "Because of the Easter Bunny!"*) I'm hopping because it's Easter, Jesus is alive, and I'm happy. Sometimes we go to church and we talk about being happy that Jesus is alive, but we don't always look so happy. But it's okay to be happy on the outside as well as the inside. Let's all hop together. (*Invite the children to hop with you for a few seconds, and then have them sit back down.*)

Okay, one more egg. Where do you think it is? (*The children will point it out to you. Go get the egg and open it as you walk back to the children.*)

Here's the third egg. Still no chocolate. It's another note, and this one says, "Don't forget the basket." Of course, the basket. How could I forget? (*Pick up the basket.*) Do you know why I have this Easter basket? (*The children will feel quite certain, "Because of the Easter Bunny!"*)

The Easter Bunny? I think you kids are just trying to confuse me. I'm holding this basket as a reminder that one of the best ways we can celebrate Jesus is by living the way he wants us to live. He taught his friends to share what they had with others.

Even kids can do their part. Once there was a boy with a basket not unlike this one. He shared his lunch of bread and fish, and it ended up feeding over 5,000 people!

CLOSING

Let's keep our Easter celebration going with our closing prayer. It's a call-and-response prayer. Whenever I say a part, you respond by saying "Hallelujah, hallelujah! Hop, hop, hop!" And when you say, "Hop, hop, hop," hop in place three times. Let's practice your part once. (*Lead the children once through their response.*)

Thank you, God, for this great day.
Hallelujah, hallelujah! Hop, hop, hop!
Thank you, God, for your great love.

Hallelujah, hallelujah! Hop, hop, hop!
Thank you, God, for your great son.
Hallelujah, hallelujah! Hop, hop, hop!
Amen.

That Extra Wow Factor

The basket can be full of plastic eggs containing Easter-related Bible verses or bracelets with inspirational messages. These can be handed out to the children at the end of the children's moment. At our church, I enlisted some volunteers to hide eggs in the children's classrooms while they were in the worship space. Near the end of the children's moment I informed all the kiddos that an Easter egg hunt was awaiting them when they got back to their Sunday school rooms. Surprise!

Embracing Rather Than Avoiding

An Easter egg hunt? The Easter Bunny? Mark, aren't these secular images? Does Jesus not even get top-billing in church?

Here's the way I look at it. Many, if not most, of the kids are thinking about egg hunts, baskets full of chocolate, and the Easter Bunny. I could try to compete with those images, or I could use those images to my advantage. I had the attention of the children, all 90 of them, throughout the children's moment. And next time the children think about egg hunts and the Easter Bunny, some of them (maybe only a handful) will make a sacred connection.

WHiCH WaY?

THeMe
While there is usually more than one way to get somewhere, having a dependable guide to follow can make the journey smoother. The most dependable guide on our journey of faith is Jesus.

SCRiPTURe
John 14:1-7 — The Way, the Truth, the Life

PRePaRe
Use a dowel and a piece of paper to a make a flag with the words, We Can Depend on Jesus. *Recruit a minister (preferably the senior minister if he or she has a playful spirit) to be the dependable guide. Recruit another adult volunteer to be a true follower. Recruit a third volunteer to hold the flag somewhere in the worship space, preferably far away from where the kids gather for the children's moment.*

In THe MoMent
It's a wonderful world, but it sure is big! It's not always easy for us to find our way around. It's a good thing we have dependable people we can count on to lead us.

Let's try a little experiment. First I'd like to welcome our good friend Darwin who's going to help us out. Everyone say "hi" to Darwin. *(Darwin is a puppet the kids know and love. He's practically an old friend.)*

Darwin enters and says hello to the kids.

Now we need a dependable person to help us out. Dr. B, *(our senior minister, Dr. Bruster),* will you help us out? *(Dr. B comes down.)*

Okay. We are looking for a flag here in the worship space, and our dependable leader Dr. B knows the way. So let's find that flag.

The volunteer with the flag holds it up. Dr. B heads for the flag with Darwin, the true follower, right behind. The two of them can make small talk as they walk. I stay up near the children, then say,

I think I'm going to find the flag on my own. Besides, I know a shortcut.

Head the opposite direction. This may very well be met with protests from the children. That would be great. In our worship space I was able to wander around for a while. I even made it up into the choir loft, asked the choir where the flag was, and 30 people pointed in 30 directions. Milk the whole wandering thing for a while then, finally, see the flag and go over to it. Get the flag and come back to the children with the other adult volunteers. It would be best for the one who truly followed the dependable leader to be the one to bring the flag back. Darwin couldn't quite hold the flag with his little puppet hands, so I brought it back for him.

Well, I got to the flag — eventually. But Darwin followed our dependable leader, Dr. B, and he got there much quicker, and without getting lost. There's usually more than one way to get somewhere, but following a dependable leader we can trust helps us so much.

And look, our flag has a message on it. It says, "We can depend on Jesus." When it comes to learning about God's amazing love, no one is more dependable to lead the way than Jesus.

CLOSING
Invite the children to join you in the following prayer by responding to each of your lines with the phrase from the flag: We Can Depend on Jesus.

Through the good times and the bad,
We can depend on Jesus.
Through the happy and the sad,
We can depend on Jesus.
When we wander to and fro,
We can depend on Jesus.
When we're not sure where to go,
We can depend on Jesus.
Amen.

A WARM WELCOME

THEME

In many worship spaces an usher or greeter is at every door. They may be the first person we see as we go to worship, and their role is important.

SCRIPTURE

John 10:1-10 — The Gate for the Sheep

PREPARE

The centerpiece for this children's moment is an interview with an usher or greeter. It is important to ask, many days in advance, the usher you'd like to interview during the service. Once you have confirmed an usher to interview, make sure she or he knows the questions you will ask. I only asked a few; these appear in the children's moment below. Also, there is an opportunity for the ushers to come forward and have the children bless them. Make sure the ushers and greeters know this in advance. Before we invite them down for the blessing, ask the ushers and greeters to stand by the doors at the beginning of the children's moment.

In the Moment

Let's all put on our eye-spy glasses. *(Have the kids put on their pretend eye-spy glasses.)* Our worship space has a lot of doors. Let's see how many doors we can spy. *(The children look through their eye-spy glasses and count the doors. This is the cue for the ushers and greeters to wave.)*

Do you see something or someone at each door? *(The children will respond, "People waving to us." The confidence of their response will depend in large part on how energetically the ushers and greeters wave.)*

Those waving people are our ushers and greeters. When we enter this worship space, we see more than a door — we see a very important person who helps make our worship experience the best it can be. I'd like us to take a moment to visit with one of our ushers.

Invite the usher to join you with the children. This is a good day to use a hand-held microphone. The usher I chose to interview was Mr. Pinkerton. He is a very kind older man who stands near the door where most of the children enter. He is a familiar face to them, and he and the children have really struck up quite a rapport. In fact, when I recently asked my youngest daughter what she likes about church, one of the things she said was, "Getting to see Mr. Pinkerton." Now, if that's not validation for the impact our ushers and greeters can have, I don't know what is.

This is Mr. Pinkerton, one of our ushers. Everyone say, "Hello, Mr. Pinkerton." *(The children do, quite enthusiastically.)*

Mr. Pinkerton, I wanted to ask you a couple of questions. When someone walks in through our sanctuary doors, what do you do?

I handed the microphone to Mr. Pinkerton. He mentioned many things, including offering a smile, a friendly greeting, and handing every person a bulletin. Each usher or greeter will have something different to say. Since I wanted the usher I chose to be able to speak freely without my feeding them lines, I was intentional about the usher I chose.

Why do you choose to serve as an usher? Is it because you get paid a lot of money?

I handed the microphone back to Mr. Pinkerton. He talked about how much the church meant to him and serving as an usher was one way of giving back. He also talked about how important he felt it was to make every single person who walked through our doors feel welcomed, accepted, and loved. I couldn't have written a lovelier response if I'd tried.

Now I'd like to invite all the ushers and greeters to come forward. *(A couple of ushers remained in the back to make sure that if someone else came in during this time, they would still be greeted and welcomed. Now that's dedication.)*

CLOSING

Ushers and greeters, if you will go right up to the children. And children, if you will reach out and hold an usher's hand, or put your hand on an usher's shoulder.

Children, will you please repeat these words as we say a special blessing for our ushers and greeters?

Dear God,
Thank you for these people
Who truly serve you
By making all of us

Feel welcomed,
Accepted,
And loved.
Amen.

ADDED BENEFITS

A children's moment is supposed be for the children, yet there are often added benefits which are undeniable. This particular children's moment taught the children while lifting up a very important ministry in our church.

THE CREATION

THEME
God created a wonderful world. We are part of God's wondrous creation.

SCRIPTURE
Genesis 1:1-31; 2:1-4 — The Creation

In the Moment
Teach the refrain – "And God saw, and God saw, and God saw that it was good. Hey!" You can sing it to a simple melody or speak it. Draw out the first two words — "And God…" while patting your thighs a la a drum roll. Then for the rest of the words — "…saw, and God saw, and God saw that it was good. Hey!" Clap to the steady beat. Throw your arms in the air on "Hey!"

Day 1— In the beginning God made the heavens and earth. And the earth was dark and shapeless. Then God said, "Let there be light." And there was light. (*Children sing the word "light" on one high pitch.*) God separated the light from the darkness, called the light "day" and the darkness "night."

All do the refrain.

Day 2 — God said, "Let there be a dome to separate the water on the ground from the water in the sky." That way there can be snow and rain. (*Lead the children and congregation to make rain by doing what you do. Start by snapping. Change to patting lightly then more heavily. Next, change to clapping. Stay with loud clapping for a few seconds, then change to heavy patting, then to light patting, then to snaps, then stop.*)

All do the refrain.

Day 3 — God said, "Let the water on the ground be gathered together. And let the dry land appear." God called the dry land "earth" and the water "sea." (*Lead the children and congregation to do the wave.*)

Then God covered the earth with plants, grasses, roses, apples, and broccoli. If you could be a tree, what kind of tree would you be. (*Invite each child to pretend to be their favorite tree.*)

All do the refrain.

Day 4 — God said, "Let there be all kinds of light in the sky." (*Lead the children to do the actions as you say each thing God created: Sun — hands to side of face; Moon — arms in circle over head; Stars — finger bursts in air.*)

All do the refrain.

Day 5 — God said, "Let the seas be filled with swimming creatures." And God made the: (*After saying each sea creature, demonstrate the sound and motion. Invite everyone to join you. Goldfish – lip pops; Squid – arms out in all directions; Shark – jaws theme, munch-munch.*)

And God said, "Let the sky be filled with flying creatures." And God made the: (*After saying each bird, demonstrate the sound and a simple motion, and invite everyone to join you: Parrot — caw-caw; Duck — quack-quack; Penguin — strain but can't fly, oh well…waddle-waddle.*) It was a busy day.

All do the refrain.

Day 6 — God said, "Let the earth be filled with all kinds of creatures. And God made the: (*After saying each land animal, demonstrate the sound and a simple motion, and invite everyone to join you: Cow — moo; Kangaroo — boing - boing; Elephant — trumpet blast.*) And God made people like you and me to care for this big, beautiful world.

All do the refrain.

Day 7 — God rested. (*Snore.*)

All do the refrain.

CLOSING
Invite the children to turn to one another and say these words.

God made the whole world.
And God made you.
And God saw that it was good.
Amen.

SEVEN DAYS IN FIVE MINUTES
I've done this children's moment in a few different settings, and it always connects, big time. It can take a fair amount of time, but then again, it is the whole creation.

THe STILL, SMALL VOICE

THEME
Sometimes the strongest messages come from the softest voices.

SCRIPTURE
1 Kings 19:1-18 — The still, small voice

IN THE MOMENT
Invite children to participate in the actions of the story.

Once there was a man named Elijah — a prophet of the Lord, who ran away into the wilderness. (*Run in place.*) He came to rest under the shade of a tree. He felt scared and alone, and wondered if it wouldn't be better if he just died. Then, exhausted, Elijah fell asleep. (*Snore.*) The Lord woke Elijah and told him, "Go stand on the mountain. I am about to pass by."

A great wind arose that split mountains and broke rocks. (*Make wind sounds.*) But the Lord was not in the wind. Next came an earthquake. (*Make rumbling sounds by patting thighs and stomping feet very fast.*) But the Lord was not in the earthquake. Then came a fire. (*Make "tss" sizzling sound as if touching something hot.*) But the Lord was not in the fire. Then there was silence. (*Have a few seconds of complete silence.*) And in the silence, Elijah heard the voice of the Lord. "Elijah." (*Gently sing "Elijah" to your own little three-note melody.*) "I need you to go back to work for me."

And Elijah went. He knew that through every storm, earthquake, or fire, God would always be near. God's love would always be near.

CLOSING
Invite the children to repeat after you. Say each successive line softer.

Help me be softer, Lord!
Help me be softer, Lord!
Help me be softer, Lord.
Help me be softer, Lord…
So I can hear you better. Amen.

WaLKinG to EMMaUS

THEME
Jesus is alive.

SCRIPTURE
Luke 24:13-35 — The Walk to Emmaus

In THE MoMent
Cue the children that when they hear bad news they say, "Aw" and when they hear good news they say, "Yay!"

One day two of Jesus' disciples were walking to the village of Emmaus. They were sad because Jesus had died. **Aw.** While they were walking and talking, Jesus came along and walked beside them. **Yay!** But the disciples did not recognize him. **Aw.** Jesus asked what they were talking about. They told him about how their Lord had died and was buried. **Aw.** But that on the third day women went to the tomb. The tomb was empty and angels told the women that Jesus was alive. **Yay!** But the disciples said, "We haven't seen Jesus, so we don't think we believe the women." **Aw.** Then Jesus reminded them of all the important things God's prophets said that had come true. **Yay!** But by then they'd come to the end of their journey. **Aw.** So the friends invited Jesus to their house to have supper. **Yay!** But they still didn't recognize him. **Aw.** Jesus sat down, took the bread, blessed it, and broke it. Immediately the disciples recognized him. **Yay!**
And then Jesus disappeared. **Aw.** But now they knew that Jesus was alive, and they spread the good news. **Yay!**

CLOSING
Invite the children to repeat after you each line of the following prayer.

Loving God,
Open our eyes,
That we may see your love.
Open our ears,
That we may hear your love.
Open our hearts,
That we may know Jesus lives.
Hallelujah, Amen.

serve

THEME
Each of us can serve in our own special way.

SCRIPTURE
Acts 6:1-7 — The Seven Helpers

PREPARE
For this children's moment you will need to be able to teach the sign for "serve." There are many great online sign language dictionaries, including www.aslpro.com and www.signingsavvy.com.

In the Moment
Today we're going to experience a story of some of the earliest church leaders in the Christian faith. First I need to teach you some sign language. This is the sign for the word "serve." *(Demonstrate the sign. It would be even better if you have someone in your congregation who is knowledgeable in sign language and willing to help out. Invite the children to sign "serve" a few times.)* Great. Now listen closely, I need your help to tell this story. Every time you hear me say the word "serve," "served," or "serving" I want you to make the sign for "serve." Here we go!

After Jesus went into heaven, his disciples continued to devote themselves to **serving** God. They **served** God by healing the sick. And they **served** God by preaching and praying. One day the disciples learned that some of the widows in the community were not getting enough food to eat. Who would **serve** them? The disciples were so busy **serving** through healing, preaching, and prayer that they couldn't do it all by themselves. They needed help. So they chose seven helpers to **serve** God by going out to help the widows have enough to eat. So many good people **serving** God and God's people — So many ways to **serve** — How will you **serve** God today?

CLOSING
Invite the children to sign the word "serve" in the following prayer.

Loving God,
With our hearts, we will **serve** you.
With our minds, we will **serve** you.

With our hands, we will **serve** you.
We will **serve** you, and **serve** your people. Amen.

Jesus Calls

THEME
Jesus asked his new friends to follow him. He first showed them what a special friend he could be for them.

SCRIPTURE
Luke 5:1-11 — Jesus Calls the Disciples

In the Moment
Today we're going to experience a story full of good things and bad things. When you hear a good thing, say, "Amen!" And when you hear a bad thing, say, "Aw, man!"

One day Jesus was standing by a lake, ready to teach about God's love. **Amen!** But the crowd was really pushing in on him to hear what he had to say. **Aw, man!** Jesus saw two boats at the shore. He got into Simon's boat. They pushed off from shore so more people could see and hear Jesus. **Amen!** When Jesus had finished teaching, he told Simon, "Go into the deeper water, and lower your nets. You'll catch plenty of fish." **Amen!** Simon answered, "Master, we have been fishing all night, and haven't caught a single fish." **Aw, man!** "But if you say so, we'll give it a try." When they had done this, they caught a LOT of fish. **Amen!** They caught so many fish that their nets started to break. **Aw, man!** Their partners in another boat came to help them. **Amen!** But there were so many fish, that both the boats began to sink. **Aw, man!** When Simon saw all of this, he got on his knees and said, "Go away from me Lord, I am a sinful man!" **Aw, man!** Simon and his partners James and John were amazed at all the fish they caught. **Amen!** Then Jesus told Simon, "Do not be afraid; from now on you will be catching people." They pulled their boats up on the shore, left everything, and followed Jesus to go make friends. **Amen!**

CLOSING
Have the children repeat after you each line of the following prayer.

Through all the good times,
And all the bad times,
We will follow Jesus.
Jesus is our friend.
Amen.

ADAM AND EVE...

AND ONE SNEAKY SERPENT

THEME

Learn to recognize when something is trying to pull us away from God's way. Also a good lesson on tattling versus telling.

SCRIPTURE

Genesis 3:1-24 — Adam, Eve, and the First Big Mistake

PREPARE

Using card stock and markers, make six signs reading:

1. Sss.	2. Hmm.	3. Munch, munch, munch.
4. duh-duh-DUH!	5. Yoo-hoo.	6. Uh-oh.

This children's moment is like an old melodrama, where the children participate by saying what is on a certain sign at the appropriate time. If you like, you can have six volunteers hold the signs for you and lift them at the appropriate times in the story.

IN THE MOMENT

Everything was going perfectly in the garden of Eden until one day, the serpent slithered by. The serpent was one crafty animal. He was sly. He was sneaky. He was slick. **Sss.** He said to Eve, "Excuse me. Did God say you couldn't eat the fruit from any of the trees in the garden?"

Eve said, "We can eat from any tree in the garden...except for that tree in the middle. And we can't touch it either."

But the serpent was suave. He was slithery. He was smooth. **Sss.** "You won't die. God knows that when you eat that fruit your eyes will be open. You'll know everything. You'll be like God."

Eve thought about that. The fruit on the tree sure looked yummy. **Hmm.** And the tree was beautiful to look at. **Hmm.** And if she ate some of the fruit, she would know everything. **Hmm.**

So Eve took some fruit and ate it. **Munch, munch, munch.** And she gave some of the fruit to Adam, and he ate it. **Munch, munch, munch.**

And at that moment they realized (almost like a bad dream) they weren't wearing any clothes. **duh-duh-DUH!** *(very dramatically each time)*

So they made some clothes out of fig leaves — fig leaf shirts, fig leaf socks, fig leaf underpants. That's when Adam and Eve heard God walking through the garden looking for them. **Yoo-hoo.** So they hid. **Yoo-hoo.**

God said, "Adam? Eve? Where are you?" **Yoo-hoo.**

Adam said, "Well, we heard you coming and we were a little embarrassed. You see…we didn't have any clothes."

"Wait a second," said God. "Who told you that you didn't have any clothes? Did you eat something you weren't supposed to?"

Adam answered, "Um…it was the woman you gave to me. She gave me fruit from the tree." **duh-duh-DUH!**

Eve said, "The serpent tricked me. It was all *his* fault." **duh-duh-DUH!**

The serpent was crafty…but he couldn't outsmart God. **Sss.**

God turned to Adam and Eve. "Let's have a little chat about natural consequences." **Uh-oh.** "So, you want to know everything, do you? Well, now you're going to know about hard work and sweat." **Uh-oh.** "And you're going to know about aches and pains." **Uh-oh.** "Now it's time for you both to leave the garden. It's all just a little too easy in here."

But God still loved Adam and Eve and made them some regular clothes because fig leaves are scratchy. **duh-duh-DUH!**

CLOSING
Invite the children repeat after you each line of the following prayer.

Dear God,
Sometimes your way is fun.
Sometimes your way is difficult.
But we will try our best,
To follow your way.
Amen.

THE BIRTH OF JESUS

A SOUND STORY

THEME
Jesus was born for all.

SCRIPTURE
Luke 2:1-20 — Jesus Is Born; Matthew 2:1-12 — The Wise Men Visit Jesus

PREPARE
You can use a white poster board and colors to make a story poster that includes a picture of each animal or person in the story. Beneath the picture of each person or animal write the corresponding sound.
Here are the sounds:

Baby — goo-goo
Mary — Away in a manger, no crib for a bed. (sing)
Joseph — Gotta take care of the baby.
Donkey — hee-haw
Cow — moo
Shepherds — Yikes!
Sheep — baa
Angels — Be not afraid.
Wise Men — Gifts for the king!

IN THE MOMENT
Show the children the story poster. Practice by pointing to each picture and having the children make the corresponding sound. Invite them to listen for each person and animal in the story. When one is mentioned, point to the picture of it and have the children make the sound. You may choose to recruit a volunteer to hold the poster and give you more freedom to move.

In those days the emperor made a decree that everyone in the empire should be counted. This meant that everyone had to go to their hometowns to register.

Joseph had to go to his hometown, the City of David, called Bethlehem. **Joseph** was engaged to **Mary** who was expecting a **baby**.

The two of them went to Bethlehem, **Mary** rode on the back of a **donkey**.

When **Mary** and **Joseph** arrived in Bethlehem, they found that there was no room for them in the inn. **Mary** and **Joseph** had to stay in a stable that was home to a **cow**. And this is where the **baby** was born. **Mary** wrapped the **baby** in swaddling clothes and laid him in the manger of the **cow**. The **donkey** rested in the nice warm hay.

Meanwhile, there were **shepherds** in the nearby fields, keeping watch over their **sheep** by night. An **angel** appeared to them and said, "Be not afraid, for I bring you good news of great joy. For to you is born this day in the City of David a Savior, Christ the Lord. You will find the **baby** wrapped in bands of cloth, lying in a manger." And suddenly there were more **angels** praising God and saying, "Glory to God in the highest, and peace to all on earth."

When the **angels** left, the **shepherds** said, "Let's go to Bethlehem to see the **baby**." So the **shepherds** ran with the **sheep** all the way to Bethlehem, and found **Mary, Joseph,** and the **baby**. The **donkey** and the **cow** were there, too.

After a time there came **Wise Men** from the east. The **Wise Men** were following a star in search of a savior that the prophets had predicted. When the **Wise Men** arrived in Bethlehem they found Jesus. And there they laid before him gifts of frankincense, myrrh, and gold.

CLOSING
Close by leading the children in singing the first verse of "Away in a Manger."

Away in a manger, no crib for a bed,
The little Lord Jesus laid down his sweet head.
The stars in the sky looked down where he lay,
The little Lord Jesus, asleep on the hay.

UP TO YOU
If you don't like mixing the Luke and Matthew stories, that's cool. You can simply end the story before the paragraph regarding the Wise Men.

LiGHt OF tHE WORLD

THEME
One person can make a difference, even when it doesn't seem that way.

SCRIPTURE
John 8:12 — The Light of the World

PREPARE
This children's moment hinges on having one child who is willing to sing the first verse of "This Little Light of Mine" by himself or herself in front of the congregation. It's a good idea to secure this child several days in advance. Make sure to practice the entire children's moment, including the solo verse, in the worship space prior to the service. It's one thing to be able to sing in a choir room; but a large sanctuary can be intimidating to even the most secure singers. And if you use microphones make sure to test everything. If you're lucky enough to have a sound engineer for worship, make sure the sound engineer is aware of when the child will sing and which microphone will be needed.

In tHE MOMEnt
We live in a bright, beautiful world. But not everything is bright. We've all heard dark words — things people have said that maybe made us feel bad or hurt our feelings.

Here's an example — I think anyone can sing. But I've talked to so many people who are afraid to sing because someone told them, "You can't sing. Don't even try." *Can't* and *don't try* — those are dark words.

Here's another example — There are people who think children are too young or small to do anything important. "A child change the world? Impossible." *Impossible* is another dark word.

Let's try a little experiment. We're going to divide the worship space into three sections.

Invite the congregation to participate in this. Indicate what the three sections are in your particular worship space.

Each section is going to murmur, not too loudly, a dark word or phrase. Section One, please start murmuring the word "Can't." (*Encourage the*

people in Section One. This will be an unfamiliar experience for most.)
Those in Section One, continue to murmur your word while those in
Section Two murmur "Don't try." Keep murmuring over and over.

Section Three, please join the people in the other two sections. Your dark
word is "Impossible."

*Continue to help the congregation keep murmuring. At this point, the child
singer, who is with the other children in the children's moment will walk to the
microphone, perhaps at a pulpit, and sing the first verse of "This Little Light of
Mine," a cappella. Now, this is important to keep in mind — the congregation is
doing their thing, and the child is doing his or her thing. At this moment, you
have little control of what happens next. In that sense, calling this an
"experiment" is truthful. In our case, the most beautiful thing happened — as
soon as the child started singing, the murmuring completely stopped. The entire
congregation was still as one child's voice sang in a worship space that seats
nearly 1,200. It was stunning. And afterward the child's beautiful singing, not
to mention courage, was met with spirited applause.*

All those voices. All those words of darkness. And one person — one
child — was able to chase that darkness away with a song of hope. That's
good news.

And do you know what else is good news? Jesus said that he was the light
of the world. And he also said that we are the light of the world. So if the
light of one child of God can chase away all those words of darkness, just
think what an entire church full of children of light could do. Let's find out.

CLOSING
For our closing today, let's all join together — kids, congregation, clergy,
choir — in singing "This Little Light of Mine."

This little light of mine, I'm gonna let it shine.
This little light of mine, I'm gonna let it shine.
This little light of mine, I'm gonna let it shine.
Let it shine. Let it shine. Let it shine.

RISK/REWARD
There was some risk involved in giving control of the children's moment
over to a child singer and the congregation. It could have fallen flat. But it
didn't. It was one of the most inspirational children's moments I've ever
been fortunate enough to be a part of. Sometimes you've just got to go for
it, and whatever happens…happens.

FiLL US UP

THEME
Sometimes we can feel very empty inside and will look for things to fill us up. Only God's love can truly make us feel full.

SCRIPTURE
John 6:25-35 — I Am the Bread of Life.

PREPARE
For this children's moment you will need to create the impression of three different stores in the worship space. First, make three large colorful signs:

1. *Sweets*   2. *Ties*   3. *Gizmos*

Next, collect three medium-size cardboard boxes or plastic bins. Shoeboxes work very well for this. Inside one box put a few pieces of candy. In another box place a few neckties — pre-tied and ready to be put on and worn. In the last box put a few "gizmos." I made a few out of small boxes with spoons duct-taped to the sides.

Recruit three volunteers to hold the signs and corresponding boxes in three different areas of the worship space. The signs and boxes represent the three stores you will visit during the children's moment. (Our sanctuary has a large balcony. I had one of the stores set up there. The kids love to see me run all the way up into the balcony. It contributes to the sense that you never know what will happen.)

In the Moment
Life is full of amazing people to meet and amazing things to do. But sometimes I can still feel a little empty, like something is, well…missing. I start to wonder what I can do to feel full again. One place I like to go when I feel this way is…the Sweet Shop. Did you know we have a candy store right here in the sanctuary?

This is the cue for the volunteer with the Sweets sign to hold it up for the kids to see. The kids will spot it almost immediately and show you where it is. Walk over to the Sweet Shop.

I like going to the Sweet Shop. They have so many yummy things I really like. *(Pull some of the pieces of candy out of the box and talk about how much you like them.)* Like peppermint. And fudge. Mmm.

You know, the candy makes me feel full for a little while. Then that feeling goes away. So I have to eat even more candy, and pretty soon I get a stomachache. Eating all that candy doesn't make me feel better. It makes me feel worse. When I've got a stomachache and I feel like something's missing…I like to go clothes shopping. And my favorite shop is the Tie Store. Did you know that store is right here in the sanctuary?

This is the cue for the volunteer with the Ties sign to hold it up for the kids to see. It's way up in the balcony, so up I go.

I like going to the Tie Store. They have so many cool ties — colorful ties, loud ties, ties with funky designs. *(As you say all this start putting on the pre-tied ties. After a few ties you will look pretty ridiculous. That's a good thing.)* I'll feel pretty good about myself in my new tie. But eventually I get bored with it, and pretty soon I'm back at the store for another tie. Soon I have a whole bunch of ties, but I'm not any happier than I was before. Something's missing. That's when I decide to go to the Gizmo Store. Did you know we have a Gizmo Store right here in the sanctuary?

This is the cue for the volunteer with the Gizmos sign to hold it up for the kids to see. It's back down on the floor level, so down I go.

I really like going to the Gizmo Store. Did you know that Pineapple makes an awesome gizmo? *(As you describe each gizmo, pull one out of the box to show the kids. Start with largest, then the medium, then the smallest.)* This gizmo plays all kinds of games, has 83 mega-bits of…um…stuff. *(Most in our church know I am technologically challenged.)* But just when I think I've found the one thing that can make my life complete, Pineapple comes out with something even better and smaller…the Gadget! It's got 90 mega-rams, not to mention a whole lot of buttons. Cool!

But only weeks after I get a Gadget, Pineapple releases their newest, most exciting product ever…the Widget! It's even smaller than the Gadget, with twice the bits rams, and this one even has…a pencil sharpener in the back. Awesomeness! I play with the Widget for a few weeks, but eventually the awesomeness wears off, and I feel as empty and incomplete as ever.

There's only one thing that can truly fill us up and make us feel complete — God's love. And no one shows us more about God's love through the words he said and the things he did, than Jesus. God's love is the one thing that can make us feel satisfied, complete, and full. There's just not an app for that!

CLOSING

Invite the children to repeat after you each line of the following prayer.

Loving God,
Thank you for the gift of Jesus.
When we're really hungry,
Jesus is exactly what we need.
When we're really sad,
Jesus is exactly what we need.
When we're feeling empty,
Jesus is exactly what we need.
When we remember Jesus,
And his amazing love,
We feel full.
Amen.

WHAT'S IT ALL ABOUT

Our senior minister planned a sermon series on the "I Am" sayings of Jesus recorded in John's Gospel. My first reaction was, "Oh, no!" The "I Am" sayings are all metaphors Jesus used to teach his disciples (his adult disciples) about himself and about the nature of God's love. "I am the bread of life." "I am the shepherd." "I am the true vine." "I am the light of the world." These are wonderfully descriptive and evocative images…for adults. For my concrete thinkers, on the other hand, this was going to be a challenge. I've seen a lot of children's moments go awry (and been responsible for some of those) when the leader tries to develop a message around the image — the bread, the vine, the shepherd. But that's not what it's really about. The trick is in boiling everything down to its essence.

Why did Jesus use the example of bread? What was he trying to convey to his disciples? In the above children's moment which is based on Jesus' "I am the bread of life," saying, not once do I even mention the word *bread*. It's not really about bread; it's about finding fulfillment in what really matters — God's love as revealed in Jesus. It's important to help our kids connect to the true message, not the metaphor.

One exception, in my opinion, is the imagery of light. So many children understand the light/darkness relationship on a deep, even visceral level. On the Sunday I did the children's moment based on "I am the light of the world" I polled the children to see how many use nightlights. Almost every hand went up. For most kids, especially younger ones, light = good.

WORTH REMEMBERING

THEME
Special experiences, such as baptism, Communion, or an All Saints Day service, help us remember what really matters.

SCRIPTURE
Luke 22:19 — Do this in remembrance of me.

PREPARE
The prep-work for this children's moment is all about ribbons. I did this one for the Sunday before Memorial Day. Here's what you need to prepare:

1. *One very large ribbon (with a bow) to wear around your head.*
2. *A small ribbon to tie around your finger.*
3. *A length of ribbon that can be placed on the altar. If your worship space has a Bible on the altar, the ribbon can be placed at Luke 22:19.*
4. *A long ribbon to tie around a minister's finger. This ribbon will also have a note attached to the other end reminding you where you put a special box. My note read "Dear Self. By now you've probably forgotten what it was you were trying to remember. There is a box under the piano with something special for the kids. All the best, Self."*
5. *A ribbon tied around a box containing many small boxes (one for each child).*

Prior to worship, plant the box under the piano, or wherever works best for your space. Tie or place all the ribbons where they go.

In the Moment
You are wearing a ribbon with a bow on your head. The kids are going to notice.

I'm wearing this ribbon on my head to remind me of something very important…that I have a smaller ribbon on my finger. *(Hold up the finger with the ribbon and take off the giant ribbon on your head.)*

Sometimes people tie ribbons to help them remember something. This ribbon is here to remind me to go to the altar. *(Walk to the altar.)*

This is our altar — a worship table that holds some very important things like a Communion cup, a Bible, candles — all things that help remind us of God's love.

And look, there's a ribbon right here at the altar. *(Hold up the ribbon.)* This ribbon is here to remind me that there's a ribbon tied around Page's finger! *(Page is one of our associate ministers.)*

This ribbon is tied around Page's finger because…um…because…I forgot. Oh, hey! There's a note at the end of the ribbon. I wonder what it says. Let's read it and find out. *(Read the note aloud)*

> Dear Self. By now you've probably forgotten what it was you were trying to remember. There is a box under the piano with something special for the kids. All the best, Self.

I better go to the piano and see what it is. *(Walk to the piano and pull out the big box. Untie the ribbon, open the big box and pull out one of the small boxes.)*

This is a memory box. After our closing this morning each one of you will get one of these. When you go home, you can put something in your memory box (preferably not a puppy) — that can help you remember a special time. Then, if you're ever feeling sad or alone, you can open your memory box and remember that special time. It's okay for us to feel sad from time to time. During those times it helps to remember that we have people who love us very much and a God who loves us very much.

CLOSING
Invite the children to repeat after you each line of the following short prayer.

Dear God,
Please help us
To always remember
What really matters.
Amen.

KEEPING THE WOW WHILE CUTTING COSTS
I don't do many give-aways anymore. I don't like sending the message to the children that going to church means getting stuff. Plus, we usually have 70 to 80 children each Sunday. That can get expensive. On the other hand, every once in a while, having something for the children to take with them can make a nice surprise. And a memory box is more than a cheap plastic toy. It requires each child to put in something of himself or herself, figuratively and literally. I found small boxes at a craft store, made from recycled paper. You could, however, substitute memory ribbons for the boxes. That would also keep the ribbon imagery going while making less of an impact on your budget.

A T-SHiRT FROM DaD

THEME

There are many ways to say "I love you."

SCRiPTURE

1 Corinthians 13:1-13 — The Gift of Love

PREPARE

Have a baseball card to give to each child.

In THE MOMENT

There are so many ways to say, "I love you." So many, in fact, that we might not always know when someone is saying it to us.

When I was a kid, I loved to play baseball. If I wasn't playing in a league, I was playing in the backyard, a vacant lot, anywhere. One of my big dreams was to make the Little League all-star team. I played catch every evening in the backyard with my dad. I read books about hitting. I took batting practice every chance I got. I wasn't one of the best players in the league, but I tried very hard.

At the end of one baseball season, when I knew I'd done my best, the coaches held a meeting to decide which kids would be on the all-star team. My dad was one of the coaches, so when he left the evening of the meeting, I knew exactly where he was going.

The hours passed so slowly. I kept looking at the clock and listening for the sound of his car in the driveway. Finally I heard the sound of his car, and my heart started pounding. What would he tell me? Did I finally make an all-star team?!

He walked in, and the look on his face told me before his words could — once again, I did not make the all-star team. I was so disappointed. I knew I had played the best I possibly could, and it still wasn't enough.

My dad had been holding something behind his back, and he pulled it out to show me — it was a T-shirt, one that I'd wanted for a while. He simply said, "Here son, I want you to have this." I took the shirt and went to my room. I was still too upset about not making the all-star team to care about the shirt. In a way, I even resented it, because it reminded me that I wasn't good enough to be an all-star.

But as the summer continued, I eventually got over my disappointment. And I wore that T-shirt all summer, even when I played catch in the back yard with my Dad.

It wasn't until years later that I understood what that T-shirt really was. It was my Dad's way of saying, "I love you, son. You will always be an all-star to me."

Now I have something for you. These are baseball cards. When I was a kid I used to collect these. After our closing, I'll give each one of you a card on behalf of our whole congregation. When you look at it, know that we love you and are proud of you.

CLOSING
Invite the children to repeat after you each line of the following prayer.

Dear God,
Give me the ears to hear,
Give me the eyes to see,
All the many ways
You show your love for me.
Amen.

IT'S PERSONAL
Admittedly, this is a very personal story. Every detail is true and specific to my own experiences when I was a ten-year-old boy. So the chances of someone else being able to pick up the exact story and run with it are probably rare at best. But haven't we all had experiences at least similar to this? We've all had to deal with crushing disappointments. And we've all had people show their love for us when we, for one reason or another, weren't ready to see it. Use that as the basis for your own story. Children love stories. And they will love to hear a true story about you! I don't make a habit of telling personal stories all the time, because I don't want the children's moment to be "The Mister Mark Show." But every once in a while a true story can really connect.

HOW CAN I KEEP FROM SINGING?

THEME

Even during the hardest of times, God is still there to love us and care for us. And that's something worth singing about.

SCRIPTURE

Acts 16:16-40 — Paul and Silas

IN THE MOMENT

Throughout the story the children will sing a simple refrain — the final line "...how can I keep from singing?" from the hymn of the same name. The complete hymn can be found in The Faith We Sing #2212. *Teach the children the refrain before starting the story.*

Paul and his friend Silas travelled from place to place telling others about God's love.

How can I keep from singing?

But some people did not like the things Paul and Silas had to say. The leaders were especially mad. They liked everything just the way it was.

How can I keep from singing?

The leaders said that Paul and Silas were disturbing the city. They had Paul and Silas arrested and thrown in the deepest, darkest jail cell of all.

How can I keep from singing?

They even put Paul and Silas in chains so they couldn't escape. But the whole time Paul and Silas knew that God was with them and cared for them.

How can I keep from singing?

At about midnight, Paul and Silas prayed and sang songs of praise to God, while the other prisoners listened. Even in prison Paul and Silas were spreading the good news of God's amazing love!

How can I keep from singing?

Suddenly…there was a big earthquake. *(You can have the children make rumbling sounds by stomping their feet and patting their thighs very fast.)* Immediately, wham! The doors of the jail cell flew open and everyone's chains were broken!

How can I keep from singing?

All the commotion woke up the jailer. When he saw that all the doors were opened, he became very upset. He knew he would get in trouble for all the prisoners going free. But Paul, said, "Don't worry! We are all here."

How can I keep from singing?

The jailer fell down trembling before Paul and Silas. They could have run away when they had the chance, but they stayed. Surely the God they served was very good. The jailer took Paul and Silas out of the jail and asked them what he could do to be saved. They told him to believe in Jesus.

How can I keep from singing?

The jailer was so grateful. He brought Paul and Silas to his own house. They ate together and the jailer and his family were all baptized. In the morning the leaders apologized to Paul and Silas for arresting them unfairly and let them go. Paul and Silas left and continued travelling from place to place, sharing the good news.

How can I keep from singing?

CLOSING
Invite the children to once again sing the refrain after you say this brief closing prayer.

Dear God,
Help us to know
That through the good times
And the bad times,
You are always with us,
You always care for us,
And you always love us.

How can I keep from singing?

WHat Love can Do

THEME
The power of God's love can transform something for the good.

SCRIPTURE
Isaiah 2:4 — Swords into plowshares; see also Genesis 50:20 — God intended it for good.

PREPARE
Acquire an egg of Silly Putty for each child.

In the Moment
It was the middle of World War II, and there was a shortage of rubber. Scientists and inventors all over the country were busy in their labs, trying to find a way to make rubber using different chemicals.

One of these inventors was James Wright. He found a way to make a kind of synthetic rubber and sent samples of it to inventors all over the world to see if they could find a use for it. None of them could find any use for it at all. It could bounce like rubber, but it was just too gooey.

Then a woman saw some of the synthetic rubber, and she had an idea – it could be packaged in small portions, and sold in her toy store. It became a hit. You could bounce it, squish it, mold it, stretch it, and even mash pictures from the comics onto it. The war would eventually end, but Silly Putty would go on to delight children for decades!

Now God may not have invented Silly Putty, but God's love is a very powerful force. It's the kind of force that can help a person see something that was intended for war and turn it into a toy that children enjoy to this very day.

I have something for you. After our closing, each one of you will get a package of Silly Putty. *(Big cheer from the kids)* But I'm not giving this to you so you can have just another toy. After worship when you take it out and play with it, stretch it, squish it, mold it, or shape it, I want you to remember the power of God's love. It makes great things happen.

CLOSING

Have the children repeat after you each line of the following prayer.

Thank you, God,
For your powerful love.
There's nothing it can't do.
Amen.

WHAT A YEAR

A few years ago I did a children's moment on the same Isaiah passage. That time I told the story of how the Slinky was invented. Both the Slinky and Silly Putty were invented in 1943, both were originally intended for use in World War II, and both ended up being transformed into children's toys. What a year!

ALL WE NEED

THEME
God gives us all we need, including a strong mind, and a loving heart.

SCRIPTURE
1 Peter 3:15-16 — Defending our faith with gentleness

In the Moment
God gives us everything we need. For example, God gives us a tough mind to help us think about things. Having a tough mind doesn't make you mean. In fact, having a tough mind can help us be nice when others try to challenge what we think or believe. When we've really thought things through, we're confident in our beliefs, and we're not so easily flustered.

Say, "Tough mind." (*Have the kids say this as they also point to their heads. Do this a few times so the kids feel confident.*)

God also gives each of us a tender heart. Just having a tough mind isn't enough. It's one thing to think through things and have confidence in our beliefs. But it's also important to have love in our hearts for others, even those who may disagree with us.

Say, "Tender heart." (*Have the kids say this as they also pat their chests. Do this a few times.*)

Now say, "Tough mind, tender heart." (*Have them say this a few times as they do the motions.*)

God also gives us helping hands. It's one thing to feel love. It's another thing to show love. Our helping hands can pat someone on the back who's had a bad day. Our helping hands can clear the dinner table or even put money in the collection plate during worship.

Say, "Helping hands." (*Have the kids say this as they also making flashing hands a la "jazz hands." Do this a few times.*)

Now say, "Tough mind, tender heart, helping hands." (*Have them say this a few times as they do the motions.*)

And God gives us moving feet. It's great to help out around the house and the church. God also wants us to go into the world and help our neighbors across the street, across town, and across the world.

Say, "Moving feet." *(Have the kids say this as they also stomp in place twice. Do this a few times.)*

Now say, "Tough mind, tender heart, helping hands, moving feet." *(Have them say this several times, and even build. This cumulative chant creates a really cool and catchy rhythm.)*

CLOSING
Invite the children to repeat after you each line of the following prayer.

Tough mind, tender heart,
Helping hands, moving feet,
Thank you God with all our souls,
For making us complete!
Amen.

A Child Shall Lead

Theme
Children can do amazing things, including lead our church.

Scripture
Isaiah 11:6-9 — The Peaceful Kingdom; see also Proverbs 20:11 — Even children make themselves known by their works.

In the Moment

There are plenty of opportunities for movement. Putting on helmets. Getting in the time machine. Pretending to go back in time can be done by having the kids stand, wave their arms, and make computer-y sounds. As you lead, allow for participation on the part of the children wherever possible.

Today we're going on a big adventure. Everyone put on your helmets. We're going for a ride in a time machine! Let's set the dials for five years ago. Okay, now let's all get in our time machine. Don't forget to buckle your seatbelts. Here we go. (*Travel back in time five years. Well, pretend to anyway.*)

Here we are in this very sanctuary five years ago. But there are no children up here at the front. Because five years ago there was no children's moment in our service. Can you believe that? But people in our church believed that worship is just as important for children as it is for adults. So they decided our service needed a children's moment. But on the first Sunday we tried it, the children were the ones who led the way. It was only a few children at first, and they were pretty nervous about coming all the way to the front of the sanctuary by themselves, trying something for the first time. But they did it. And then week by week, month by month, more children started coming forward, until five years later it was all of you.

This is obviously quite specific to our church. Look into your own church's worship history to see how far back you would have to set the dials to go to a time when there was no children's moment. If your church has simply always had a children's moment, I don't know what to tell you other than…that's awesome.

Let's get back in our time machines. This time let's set the dials for 33(ish) A.D. That's a long time ago. Here we go. (*Travel back in time to 33 A.D.*)

Here we are during the time of Jesus. And there's Jesus over there teaching. Some children want to come to see him and many of the grownups around Jesus are getting upset by this. But Jesus says to let the children come to him. That's wonderful news. Now think about this — it was children and those who truly love children who once again led the way. Someone had to be brave enough to be the first to approach Jesus while the grownups around frowned their disapproval.

Let's get back in our time machines and go even further back in time, to around 700 B.C. (*Travel back in time to 700 B.C.*)

This is during the time of one of the great prophets, a man named Isaiah. Some of the most beautiful and inspiring passages in the entire Bible are from Isaiah. He foretold of a time when there would be no more fighting or war. Everyone would live in peace. And here's the thing — he said that the one who would lead the way would be…a child.

Well, we've had fun in the past, but now it's time to return back to the present before our families start to wonder where we are. (*Travel back to the present.*)

Well, here we are, back in our sanctuary in the now. It was fun to go back and see all those amazing children leading the way to a better world. And you know what? You are amazing children, too. Now is your time. I know you will lead the way. Let's start by making our commitment to God.

Closing
Invite the children to very emphatically repeat after you each line of the following prayer.

We are not the future of this church.
We are the now of this church.
We are children of God.
We can lead the way right now.
Amen.

Soap Box Issue #1
I try not to get on too many soap boxes, but this is one I will climb on every chance I get. Can we please not refer to our children as "the future" of our church, as if their value is primarily in carrying on our legacy? They are with us right now. They are spiritual beings right now. They are part of the family of God right now. They can lead and make an impact right now!

Making Room

Theme
Making room isn't always comfortable or easy.

Scripture
Luke 2:1-7 — No room in the inn

In the Moment
Most of us know the story pretty well by now. Jesus was born in a stable because…(*Allow just enough space for the children to fill in the blank – "There was no room in the inn."*)

Right, there was no room in the inn.

I want to ask a question. If you were living in Bethlehem back then, who would have made room for Mary and Joseph and the baby Jesus? (*Most of the hands go up.*)

You know, I like to think I would have made room, too. But making room can be uncomfortable.

One Christmas my Nana and Papa were coming to stay with us. I was very excited until my mom said that Nana and Papa would be staying in my room and I'd have to share a bed with my little brother.

Already I had to make room and it wasn't even Christmas yet. So I shared a bed with my little brother. And here's the deal — he liked to sleep sideways in the bed. So the whole time I was trying to sleep, I could feel his feet digging into my ribs. It kinda tickled, kinda hurt, kinda kept me up all night.

So I got out of bed to make room for my little brother — the sideways sleeper. I went and slept on the couch. Making room was the right thing to do. That doesn't mean it was an easy thing to do.

And now it's time for your big challenge. You have a homework assignment. (*Some groans.*)

Oh, I know, and right before Christmas. Here's what I want you to think about —

Most of us are going to get toys, socks, something, for Christmas. One of the trickiest things will be finding enough room to put our new gifts somewhere. This is a problem that many children around the world simply don't have. What I'd like you to do is find something on your shelves or in your toy box that you don't play with anymore. Next Sunday I'd like you to bring that toy here for the children's moment to donate to our church's mission. *(Or find an organization in your community that accepts gently used toys.)* The toys will be given to children in our community who might not otherwise ever get a toy to play with. This will not be easy. Talk it over with your parents.

At this point I turn to the congregation where the parents are, hopefully, listening.

And parents, it is very important that the toy to give away be the child's choice. We want this to be as empowering and positive an experience for them as possible.

Back to the kids.

So think carefully about how you are going to make room by bringing one toy to next week's children's moment and donating it to our mission.

CLoSinG
Invite the children to repeat after you each line of the following prayer.

Dear God,
On Christmas we remember
To make room in our homes,
And to make room in our hearts.
Amen.

Making Christmas Last

THEME
Making Christmas last is about continuing to give, not continuing to get.

SCRIPTURE
Matthew 2:1-12 — The Gifts from the Wise Men

PREPARE
Provide large boxes or bins for collecting the toys the children bring to donate. (A woman had donated two large rolling suitcases the week prior. These were perfect for collecting toys, and luggage is very popular with the clients of our mission.) Also, there is a very good chance that some of the children were not in worship the previous week and did not bring a toy from home. Have several "back-up" toys on hand so all the children can participate. Bring a toy of your own to donate. I would never ask a child to do something like this without being willing to do likewise.

In the Moment
Well, Christmas Day has come and gone. And it can feel a little sad. I've got a carol to help cheer us up. You already know most of it. I'll sing a line and then you respond. I'm not even going to tell you what your response is, but you're so smart, you'll get it right away. And congregation, I'd love for you to join us.

This carol is to the tune of "Deck the Halls." You sing the first part of each line and indicate for the children and congregation to respond with the Fa-la-la part.

Christmas Day has come and gone.
Fa-la-la-la-la, la-la-la-la.
Can we make the joy go on?
Fa-la-la-la-la, la-la-la-la.
Yes, we can through love and caring,
Fa-la-la, la-la-la, la-la-la.
And the joy that we are sharing.
Fa-la-la-la-la, la-la-la-la.

I love Christmas, and I would really love for it to keep going. And we can keep the spirit of Christmas going, not by getting more, but by giving.

Christmas really is about giving. Besides, there's a reason they're called "gifts" instead of "gets."

I see you all have brought so many beautiful toys from home to give to the mission. And I want to tell you on behalf of the church how proud we are of you. Picking one of your own toys to donate to the mission is not easy. Know that these toys we give will brighten the day of many children in our community. Christmas isn't over. It's just begun.

Let's all bring our toys and put them in the boxes. Once you've put in your donation, we'll all gather around the boxes to say a special blessing.

Help facilitate as each child places his or her donation in the box. Allow some time for this. Not every child will be particularly eager to give up a familiar toy. Once all the toys have been placed in the box, invite the children to each place a hand on the box.

Closing
Invite the children to repeat after you each line of the following blessing as they keep their hands on the box of toys. You may choose to have the senior minister lead this.

Loving God,
Please bless these gifts.
They have brought us so much joy.
May they bring joy to others.
Amen.

Real Giving
I hadn't thought about this children's moment for a long time. One day I happened to find a video of the service and sat down to watch. During the time when I was talking the children were holding the toys they brought to donate. Some were holding them without thinking too much about it. But there were more than a few children who still visibly cared for the toys. One boy had a stuffed giraffe that he was holding very close, practically hugging. One girl was still completely interested in a ball she had brought. These children weren't merely going through some exercise. They were making a true sacrifice, giving up toys they cared for so that others could have a toy for Christmas. Children are precious and can be cute and very funny. And they also should be taken seriously.

MoRe THaN WoRDS

THeMe

It's not just what you say; it's also how you say it. It's not just what you do; it's also how you do it.

SCRiPTURe

Isaiah 35:1-10 — Everlasting joy of the redeemed

In THe MoMent

I believe that what we say is important. But there's got to be more to it than that. It's not just what we say; it's also how we say it. What we do is important. But it's not just what we do; it's how we do it.

Let's try a little experiment —

Everyone turn to your neighbor. *(Invite the whole congregation to do this.)* Now say to your neighbor…with the saddest voice possible… "Merry Christmas."

Go ahead, try it. *(There will be a lot of giggling. It's very difficult to sound "sad" on cue, especially when saying, "Merry Christmas.")*

Don't laugh. Don't even smile. This is very sad stuff. *(Most can't keep from smiling.)*

See? It's more than just saying happy words. You feel real happiness in your hearts, and that happiness wants to come out. Something on your face and in your heart makes it very difficult to say "Merry Christmas" with a sad voice.

Let's try another experiment. One of my favorite songs this time of year is "Jingle Bells." Let's all stand and sing "Jingle Bells" with sad voices and sad faces. *(Lead everyone in a very sad chorus of "Jingle Bells." There will be a lot of giggling and smiling throughout this.)*

Jingle bells, jingle bells, jingle all the way,
Oh, what fun it is to ride in a one-horse open sleigh. Hey!
Jingle bells, jingle bells, jingle all the way,
Oh, what fun it is to ride in a one-horse open sleigh. Hey!

That was pretty sad. It really didn't fit with the words. Let's try it again, this time with angry voices and angry faces.

Lead a very angry chorus of "Jingle Bells." This will look and sound even more ridiculous.

Okay, that didn't seem to fit, either. Let's try it one more time with joyful voices and joyful faces.

Lead a joyful chorus of "Jingle Bells." It's amazing how much louder and more boisterous this version is.

Wow! That was amazing. The words to "Jingle Bells" are so joyful. But it wasn't until you sang with joyful voices and joyful faces, that the true joy of the song came out! It's not just what you say; it's how you say it. It's not just what you do; it's how you do it.

CLOSING
Invite the children to repeat after you each line of the following prayer. Do the prayer three ways, once with a sad voice, once with a confused voice, and once with a joyful voice. Wait until the end of the joyful rendition to add the Amen.

Dear God,
Fill our hearts with joy.
Amen.

One Person of Faith

Theme
One person of faith can make a difference in the world.

Scripture
Hebrews 11:1 — Faith is…

Prepare
This one takes a good deal of prep-work, but it's worth it. Here are the steps.

1. *On a large manila envelope write these words:* You are a person of faith, and you can make a difference. Open this envelope and give the two small envelopes inside to two of our ministers.

2. *On two smaller envelopes write these words:* You are a person of faith, and you can make a difference. Open this envelope and do what the card tells you to do.

3. *On one small card write these words:* Take the sign beside the pulpit and hold it for the congregation to see.

4. *On a second small card write these words:* Open the little box by the pulpit and hand a slip of paper to each child seated at the front for the children's moment.

5. *Place the cards inside the smaller envelopes and place the smaller envelopes inside the large manila envelope.*

6. *Use a large piece of white poster board to make a large sign which reads —* Turn to Hymn #452. *(Hymn #452 in* The United Methodist Hymnal *is "My Faith Looks Up to Thee." This was an appropriate choice for the theme. If you use a different hymnal, modify this part as needed.) Place the sign and the little box beside the pulpit or somewhere visible near the front of your worship space.*

7. *Make many slips of paper, each with the following Person of Faith Pledge. (See page 79. You will need a slip for each hymnal in the pews. I also recommend using a bright color such as orange so the slips will really stand out.)*

Recruit several volunteers to place a slip of paper with the pledge in each pew hymnal, right at Hymn #452 (or whichever hymn you choose). Whew! That was a LOT of set-up, but it helps create a true moment of wonder.

In the Moment

(While holding the large manila envelope) Faith is very important. And faith is more than believing in God. It's also trusting that God has given each one of us the power to make a difference in this world.

Now, it's a really big world. It may be difficult for some of us to have faith that we as individuals can actually make a difference. "I'm just one person. What could I do?"

We're going to find out. It's time for an experiment. *(Choose a child volunteer to help you with this next part. It needs to be a child who can read and who you feel certain will do what the envelope says to do.)*

Thomas is one person. But Thomas is more than "just" one person. He's a person of faith, and he can make a difference. Okay, Thomas, are you ready? Here's an envelope. I leave it all in your hands.

Hand the child volunteer the envelope. The child will read the envelope, open it, and hand the two smaller envelopes to two ministers. If you do not have two or more clergy near the front, the envelopes could go to the senior minister and the choir director, or to two ushers. Adapt this as needed for your worship setting.

Thomas has read his envelope, opened it and found two smaller envelopes for two of our ministers.

It's a good idea to narrate what's going on for everyone since very few people are actually able to read what's on the envelopes and cards. The ministers look at their envelopes, open them and read what is on the cards. Then they head for the poster and small box.

Good. The ministers are following the instructions written on their cards. One is reaching for the sign, and the other is reaching for a box with slips of paper to hand to each of you.

By now the minister with the sign is holding it up while the other minister is handing out slips to the children.

Well, congregation, I think the sign is a message for you.

Little by little the adults catch on and open their pew hymnals to #452. Comments and laughter of recognition can be heard throughout the worship space as the grownups realize there's a little surprise waiting for them in their hymnals. (Even adults like surprises from time to time.) By now all the children and adults should have a slip of paper with the Person of Faith Pledge. Having all the slips in one bright color creates quite a vision once all the slips are out of the hymnals.

Look at that! It looks like everyone has a slip of paper right now. Everyone let's wave our papers in the air. *(This looks really cool.)*

Guess what, Thomas? You got all that started. One person of faith, with nothing more than an envelope, was able to make a difference.

CLꙨSiNG

Each of you has a slip of paper, and on that paper is written a Person of Faith Pledge. For our closing, let's all stand and say this pledge together. After that, you can all take the pledge home with you and put it on the refrigerator, or on your bathroom mirror, or even use it as a bookmark. Put it somewhere you can see it often and be reminded that you can make a difference. Here we go.

I am a person of FAITH
And I can make a difference.

God put FAITH in my heart
To love what I have not seen.
God put FAITH in my feet
To go where I have never been.

God put FAITH in my hands

To help people I have never met.

I may be one person,
But I am a person of FAITH.

I can make a difference.
I will make a difference –

Today!

FaitH

This children's moment was a blast. It was fun to think up, fun to put together, and fun to see in action. Now, I did some tweaking so that the one you have is much more refined. I took out a step that put too much in the hands of the adults. When we did this children's moment the children who had roles did absolutely everything the envelopes asked them to do. Guess who had a hard time following the instructions? Yep — the adults! There was a point where my faith was tested as to whether the children's moment could get back on track. I was really sweating. But despite some things that didn't quite go as I'd planned, everything worked out just fine. (Oh, me of little faith.)

BREATHE

THEME
We inhale and exhale all the time. How often do we take the time to really breathe?

SCRIPTURE
John 20:19-22 — Breathing the Holy Spirit

In the Moment
Before we start our children's moment, I wanted to give you this friendly reminder – don't forget to breathe. *(Some puzzled looks from the kids.)* I know that seems like a no-brainer, right? Don't we breathe all the time? Do we really need to go to church to learn all that?

Well, we inhale and exhale, all the time. But that isn't quite the same as really breathing.

Inhaling is when we take air into our lungs. Let's all inhale together. *(Lead the children to inhale.)*

Exhaling is when we blow air out of our lungs. Let's all exhale together. *(Lead the children to exhale.)*

I sure do a lot of inhaling and exhaling. But sometimes I think I forget to truly breathe.

Like when I'm on my way to church and I'm thinking about all the things I have to do. Inhale. Exhale. Inhale. Exhale. Then when I get to the church I have to get the coffee ready for the teachers — Inhale. Exhale. — and I need to make sure every classroom has all the materials needed — Inhale. Exhale. Then there are sign-in sheets to distribute and lessons to teach — Inhale. Exhale.

Later on I have to hurry up to the balcony and get the microphone for the children's moment. Inhale-exhale-inhale-exhale-inhale-exhale-inhale-exhale. But in those moments when I'm the most in-a-hurry, those are the times when it's most important…*(take a deep, cleansing breath)*…to breathe.

Let's all take in a deep breath together. Here we go. *(Lead the children in a deep, cleansing breath.)*

There's a real difference. Inhaling and exhaling fills our lungs with air and helps us live. But when we take the time to breathe, it fills more than our lungs, it fills our souls, and it just plain makes us feel better.

CLOSING

Lead the children to breathe in the different ways indicated throughout this interactive prayer.

Let everything that breathes praise the Lord.
(deep breath in and out)

Let the busy bee, with its
Busy buzzing breath, praise the Lord.
(buzz)

Let the slithery snake, with its
Slow, slinky breath, praise the Lord.
(hiss)

Let the cuddly kitten, with its
Curly, purr-ly breath, praise the Lord.
(purr)

Let the playful puppy, with its
Playful panting breath, praise the Lord.
(pant)

Let everything...
(inhale a little bit)

Everything...
(inhale a little more)

Everything that breathes...
(inhale a little more)

Praise the Lord!
(EXHALE)

Amen.

THE GOOD BOOK

THEME
The Bible has many difficult and challenging parts. That doesn't mean we should throw the whole thing out because we have a hard time with parts of it. Think of all the beautiful and inspiring Scripture we would miss out on.

SCRIPTURE
2 Timothy 3:16-17 — Scripture is inspired by God.

PREPARE
You will need four books: a cookbook, a book of knock-knock jokes, a pirate book, and a Bible. Or you can use prop-books that represent the ones listed.

In the Moment
I want to clear some room in my office, and I'm thinking of getting rid of some books. I have here a short stack of books that I'm considering.

(Hold up the cookbook.) Here's a cookbook. Let's take a look. *(Pretend to page through it.)* Hmm, there's a recipe for chocolate cake in here. That's good. And here's a recipe for muffins. Mm. That looks good. And…uh-oh. Here's a recipe for asparagus soufflé. Yikes! We better throw this cookbook out. *(Turn one more page.)* But wait. We can't throw this book out. It's got a recipe for apple pancakes. We better keep this book.

Let's take a look at another book and see if we can throw it out. It's a book of knock-knock jokes. *(Pick up the knock-knock joke book and pretend to flip through the pages.)* Okay, here's one. *(Do a few knock-knock jokes with the children.)*

Knock-knock. **Who's there?** Lettuce. **Lettuce who?** Lettuce tell knock-knock jokes. *(The kids laugh hysterically.)*

Knock-knock. **Who's there?** Seymour. **Seymour who?** Seymour stuff with your eyes open. *(Some laughs, and probably some groans from the adults.)*

Yeah, that one wasn't so funny. Maybe we should try one more.

Knock-knock. **Who's there?** The impatient chicken. **The impat…**Pa-GOCK!!! *(Uproarious laughter.)*

Wow! I guess I better keep this book, too. Just think. If I'd thrown it out we would've all missed out on that little bit of comic gold!

Let's try another book. *(Hold up the pirate book.)* Here's a book about pirates I was thinking of throwing out. Let's read and see what we should do. *(Pretend to read.)* Okay, well here's a part about a pirate who is sailing with his pirate mateys on the open sea. But then his ship is wrecked and he has to swim through shark-infested waters to an island where he is rescued by a princess who…oh, no! There's kissing in this book! Gross! We should definitely throw this book out. *(Turn a page.)* Oh wait. It's okay. The pirate and the princess get rescued by a spaceship and taken to the planet of the dinosaurs. Whew. It's a good thing we kept reading. Otherwise we would've thrown out a really good book. You know, maybe we should be careful about trying to throw away books just because they have a few things we don't like.

Here's one more book. *(Hold up the Bible.)* Ooh, this one is tricky. It's the Bible. This book has some of the most beautiful passages ever written. But there are also some parts that many people don't like — parts about fighting other people, for example — that make some people wonder if it wouldn't be better to just ignore the Bible completely.

Maybe we can just get rid of some parts and keep the rest. But even that can be tricky. If we turn to a page of the Bible, we can read about some of that fighting and war that we have a hard time with. *(Turn in the Bible to the page immediately after the one that contains Joshua 1:9. Then flip back one page.)* But if we turn to the other side of that page, we find one of the most inspiring passages in the entire Bible. Here are some words from Joshua 1:9 — "Have courage, be not dismayed, for the LORD your God is with you wherever you go." That is a beautiful passage, and we would have missed out on it if we had thrown away just one page of the Bible. Maybe we should be careful about throwing out books just because we don't like or agree with every word of them.

CLOSING
Invite the children to repeat after you each line of the following prayer.

Dear God,
The Bible is the Good Book,
Not the Easy Book.
Help us
To understand it better.
Amen.

WHaT GOD WaNTS FoR US

THeMe
Sometimes bad things happen. That doesn't mean God makes those bad things happen to us.

SCRiPTURe
John 11:32-37 — Jesus Weeps.

In THe MoMeNT
When I was five I got a puppy. We named her Pasha. I loved to play with Pasha, pet her, feed her, run around the yard with her.

But one thing about puppies — they have very sharp little teeth. One day I was reaching for a ball to throw for Pasha, and she reached for the ball at the same time and…ouch! She accidentally bit me on the hand. It really hurt and I started crying.

Now there wasn't a reason I got bit. It was an accident. Some people want to believe that when something bad happens to someone that they somehow deserve it, or that it's part of some big plan. I do not believe that God made Pasha bite me. But I do believe that when Pasha saw that I was crying and came over to give me puppy kisses and make sure I was okay, God was there.

When I was a little older, I was playing in my Nana's backyard. I was having a great time when a bee came and stung me on my finger. I ran crying into the house, "Nana! Nana! A bee stung me! I wasn't doing anything to it and it stung me anyway!"

I do not believe God made that bee sting me, even though God knew I'd snuck an extra cookie after dinner the night before. I just happened to be playing too close to where the bee lived. But I do believe that when Nana pulled out the stinger and kissed my finger to make it feel better, God was there.

Many years later my Papa died. I wish he had lived longer, but he didn't. After his funeral I was feeling very sad and was sitting by myself. An old friend of Papa's came and sat next to me and visited. Not one time did Papa's old friend ever say it was God's plan to take Papa. That meant so much to me, because I do not believe that God takes grandparents away from their grandchildren. But I do believe that when Papa's old friend came and told me stories about Papa when he was my age — stories that made me smile — God was there.

We live in a wonderful world where amazing things happen. And it is natural that, from time to time, bad things happen as well. Sometimes we want to explain why those bad things happen so we don't have to feel so confused or hurt. I don't believe God makes bad things happen to people. God loves us way too much. God's work is always in the good. When something bad happens, God's heart is the first to break, God's eyes are the first to shed a tear, and God's hands are the first to reach out to us, hold us, and help us know that we are loved.

Closing

Have the children repeat after you each line of the following prayer.

When the dog bites,
When the bee stings,
When I'm feeling sad,
I simply remember the power of your love,
And then I don't feel so bad.
Amen.*

*Adapted from "My Favorite Things," lyrics by Oscar Hammerstein II.

FRIENDS

THEME
Making new friends and maintaining old friendships are both important.

SCRIPTURE
Ruth 1:16 — Your people will be my people.

PREPARE
Have a construction paper heart and a crayon for each child. This children's moment involves teaching the song "Make New Friends." It's a simple song to teach and learn, and you don't have to be a great singer to teach the kids this song. If, however, teaching a song to children in front of the whole congregation would simply feel too overwhelming to you, enlist a volunteer from the adult choir, maybe even the choir director, to help you.

In the Moment
I want to teach you a very simple song. It's about making new friends, while keeping the friends we already have. I'll sing a line and you sing it back to me.

(sing) Make new friends.

The children respond, "Make new friends." If the children sound pretty confident and secure, continue with the next line. Otherwise repeat the first line and encourage the children. Also, if the children seem a little too "on the spot" singing in front of the entire congregation, have the adults sing, too.

(sing) But keep the old. *(The children echo.)*
(sing) One is silver. *(The children echo.)*
(sing) And the other gold. *(The children echo.)*

Good. Now I'll sing a little longer line this time, and I'm sure you'll get it because you are all so smart!

(sing) Make new friends, but keep the old. *(The children echo.)*
(sing) One is silver and the other gold. *(The children echo.)*

Great! You really are learning this song fast. Now let's sing the whole song together.

Lead the children, and possibly the congregation, in singing the song. Sing through the whole song twice.

Make new friends, but keep the old.
One is silver and the other gold.

Good job. Now I want to give each of you a heart and a crayon.

Hand a construction paper heart and a crayon to each child. Have a few volunteers to help make this go faster.

Here's what I want you to do — go out into the congregation and get two people to sign your heart. One signature has to be from a person you already know. The other signature should be from someone you haven't met yet. And if you are feeling a little shy and would like a parent or other grownup you know to go with you and help get your heart signed, that's okay.

And while you're getting two people to sign your heart all of us, kids and grownups, are going to sing the song we just learned. Ready? Go!

Lead all in singing "Make New Friends" as the children collect signatures on their hearts. You can also help facilitate the signing of the hearts, or have the same volunteers facilitate who helped pass out the hearts and crayons. Don't be in too much of a rush to get this done. The kids like getting the signatures on their hearts, and the grownups absolutely adore this. After a minute or two, call the children back to the front.

It's fun to make new friends. It's fun to see familiar friends. Take your hearts with you and as you look at them throughout the week, remember — you have friends, and you are a friend!

CLOSING
Invite the children to repeat after you each line of the following prayer.

Dear God,
Thank you for new friends.
Thank you for old friends.
And thank you for the greatest friend in the world,
Your son, Jesus.
Amen.

Making Popcorn

Theme
Together we can do amazing things.

Scripture
Ecclesiastes 4:9 — Two are better than one.

In the Moment
Today we're going to do something together that we simply couldn't do by ourselves.

I know many of us have "made rain" before by snapping and clapping in a large group. A bunch of people working together to do that can make a pretty realistic rain sound. But we're not going to make rain today, oh no! Today, we are going to make…popcorn.

First we need to practice making popping sounds with our mouths.

Demonstrate a few different ways to make popping sounds. You can pop your lips like a fish. You can gently pat your lips with your mouth slightly open. You can place a finger inside your mouth and flick it out quickly for a popgun sound. The idea here is to give people options for how they make popping sounds with their mouths.

I need a volunteer — someone who can be a really loud popper.

Have all the children pop together a few times, then select a child who you see can make a loud pop. Make sure the child is on board with this.

You are going to be our leader. On my signal you are going to make a popping sound, and keep making it over and over.

Then I'm going to hold my hand out and walk from one side of our worship space to the other. When you see my hand pass over where you are, start to make popping sounds, and keep it going. And grownups, we want you to join in the fun, too. Everyone pops today!

When I make it all the way across the worship space, everyone in the room should be popping. Watch as I indicate for you to get faster and pop louder.

Then, after several seconds, I will hold out my hand and walk back the other way across our worship space. When you see my hand pass over where you are, stop popping. Little by little the popping will stop until only our pop leader is left. Then when I give the signal, our leader will stop popping and we'll have a bag of freshly popped popcorn waiting for us. Ready? Here we go.

Lead everything as you explained it. Once you've gone all the way across the worship space and back again, allow the leader a few good solo pops before giving the signal to stop. This whole experience is a lot of fun, especially with a large group. It is often met with big applause and laughter.

I think it's ready. Let's open our bags, and eat some popcorn.

You know what's really cool? One person popping makes a pretty neat sound. But when we all pop together, we can do something special — make popcorn. It took all of us to do it.

CLOSING
As you speak the following prayer, have the children respond after each line by popping.

Dear God,
(pop)
Help us remember
(pop)
Together we can do
(pop)
Amazing things.
(pop)
Amen.
(pop)

FOLLOWING

THEME
We're called to follow Jesus' example. That's not always easy to do.

SCRIPTURE
Matthew 19:21 — Go sell your possessions…follow me.

In the Moment
Follow me by doing just what I do. (*Perform a series of actions for the children to do along with you. Start with something simple then gradually build to trickier actions. You can make up your own sequence, or follow this one.*)
Start by patting your tummy slowly and steadily.
Change to patting your head.
Change to patting your shoulders then…
Freeze. (Some kids may not have noticed that you froze. Remind them to watch you carefully then continue.)

Jesus asked the disciples to follow him and wants us to follow him too. Sometimes following Jesus can be easy, like when we sing songs to God or pray for friends and family.

Perform more actions and invite the children to do them with you. Remind them to watch closely. This sequence can be tricky faster.
Sway to one side then clap.
Sway to the other side then clap.
Repeat this a couple more times then…
Freeze!

Sometimes following Jesus can be really hard, like when he says we should love our enemies. He even told his disciples to sell what they owned and to give the money to the poor. Wow! That would be a really hard thing to do. That's how it is with Jesus. Following him sure isn't easy. But it's the right thing to do, and we can trust him.

CLOSING
Invite the children to repeat after you each line of the following prayer.

We will follow Jesus.
It will be easy sometimes.
It will be hard sometimes.

It will be right all the time.
Amen.

Remember Your Baptism

Theme
Baptism is a way we are reminded that God loves us, no matter what.

Scripture
Mark 1:9-11 — The Baptism of Jesus

Prepare
Make several cards (using index cards or cardstock) that read: God loves you, no matter what. *Our church has a die-cut press. Using light blue cardstock I die-cut seashells with:* God loves you, no matter what. *written on each one.*

Our worship space has two center aisles. Many people sit in pews next to these two aisles. I placed a seashell in each pew hymnal near both aisles. I placed each seashell at the hymn "Child of Blessing, Child of Promise" (#611 in The United Methodist Hymnal*). I also made sure the seashells were tucked down in the hymnals and out of sight until just the right moment.*

In the Moment
Many of you have been baptized right here in our sanctuary. Most of you were baptized as babies, making it difficult for you to remember exactly what happened. A minister, usually Dr. B *(that's how the kids lovingly refer to our senior minister, Dr. Bruster)*, held you and sprinkled some water on your head. Some of you liked that. Some of you did not, and boy did you have something to say about it!

Dr. B reminded the congregation that we come into relationship with God based not on anything we do, but because God loves us, no matter what. Then Dr. B would walk you around the sanctuary so everyone could see you. Many of you liked this part a lot. Some of you smiled. Some of you kicked your feet. Most of you were fascinated with Dr. B's beard. And let's face it — it's a pretty cool beard.

Everywhere Dr. B took you throughout the sanctuary people would wave and smile. Each wave and each smile was saying something very important – we love you, no matter what.

We're going to go on a little field trip. Don't worry. You don't need a permission slip signed by your parents. The field trip is going to be right here in our sanctuary. I would like half of you to walk over and stand in one center aisle and half of you to go stand in the other center aisle. If you get to the narthex, you've gone too far.

Give the children several seconds to do this. You may need to make sure they line the whole aisle and don't all just clump together in one bunch. Kids are expert clumpers.

Now I would like the grownups who are sitting near the center aisles to find the pew hymnals closest to the aisles. Please open those hymnals to number 611 *(or whichever hymn you choose)* and take out what you find there.

Allow several seconds for the grownups seated near the aisles to find the seashells. The adults will enjoy the surprise.

Those of you who are holding the seashell cards, I would like you to look a child in the eye and read to that child what is on your seashell.

The sound of adults telling children "God loves you, no matter what" fill the worship space. It's a moment of wonder.

Now I'd like the adults to hand those seashell cards to the children. Children, you can take the seashells home with you. At least once a day I want you to look at your card and remember that God loves you, no matter what.

CLOSING
Have the children remain in the aisles. Next, invite the rest of the congregation to repeat after you each line of the following affirmation to the children.

God loves you, no matter what.
We love you, no matter what.
Remember your baptism.
Amen.

BRICK BY BRICK

THEME
Going patiently step by step is more effective than rushing to finish something.

SCRIPTURE
Romans 8:25 — Wait for it with patience.

PREPARE
Provide three shoeboxes, each with the same number of large Legos. Put enough Legos in each shoebox, 8 to 10, to form the shape of a house — the typical triangle-on-top-of-a-square shape. The Legos should be separated within each box prior to the children's moment. Recruit a child volunteer and an adult volunteer to assist you. Give each of them a shoebox with the Legos and keep one box for yourself. Practice the flow of this children's moment, including how to build the house, with your volunteer assistants.

In the Moment
I have a couple of friends joining me today. Each of us is going to build a house out of Legos. Ready? Okay, here we go.

The adult volunteer and you struggle mightily with this. You want to get your houses built as soon as possible. You try mashing the Legos together. You try dropping Legos on top of each other. Nothing seems to work. Meanwhile, the child volunteer is very slowly, calmly putting her house together. All the while she says, "Brick by brick. Brick by brick." By the time she is almost done, the adult volunteer starts to notice her progress. He asks her how she built such a nice house, and she responds, "Brick by brick. Brick by brick."

Meanwhile, you are still engrossed in your attempts to build the house as fast as possible. The adult volunteer tries to get your attention and convince you that the child is really on to something with the whole "brick by brick" idea. But you can't be bothered. The adult volunteer starts building his house while saying, "Brick by brick. Brick by brick." The child volunteer is saying it along with him as encouragement.

Soon, both of them have their houses completely built. You are getting very frustrated, but you keep trying to build the house all at once. Then you notice that you're the only one still working. You look over to see the adult and child proudly holding their completed houses.

Hey! How did you make your houses?

They respond in unison, "Brick by brick."

Brick by brick? But that will take longer.

The child says, "Yes, but we both have our houses built."

That's a good point. Tell me again how it is you built your houses.

They respond, "Brick by brick."

Okay, brick by brick. I'll give it a try.

Start slowly building your house. The adult and child can lead the other children to chant, "Brick by brick! Brick by brick!" until you complete your house. Then all three of you proudly hold up your finished houses.

Thanks, friends. I guess I just needed to be more patient and not try to get it all finished at once. Brick by brick really is the best way to build a house.

CLoSiNG
Have the children repeat after you each line of the following prayer. Draw out the space before the word "patience" a little more each time.

Dear God,

Give us......patience.

Give us................patience.

Give us...................................patience.

Give us..patience.

Amen.

Do We Have to Go to Churh?

THEME
Going to church matters.

SCRIPTURE
1 Peter 2:10 — Now you are God's people.

In the Moment

(In your most exasperated voice) Do we have to go to church?! *(Many of the kids will answer "Yes!" You've got to give them credit. They know what they're expected to say.)*

Some Sundays the pjs feel extra cozy. The French toast is extra syrupy. The Sunday comics are extra funny. Besides, we've learned that God is with us wherever we go. Surely God is with us at home. And we learn in church that God hears our prayers no matter where we offer them. Surely God can hear our prayers while we're home in our pjs. So we have to wonder — does going to church really matter?

Let's think about that more in a minute. First, let's play a game. And I'd love for the congregation to join in so we're all playing together. I'm going to ask a few questions and if the answer for you is yes, please stand up. Everyone put on your listening ears. *(Touch your ears.)*

Here's the first question — Are you sitting near someone who you normally only see at church?

Many people stand up. Have them stay standing for a few seconds, then invite them to sit back down.

Here's the next question — When you come to church is there someone you always look forward to seeing?

Many people stand up. Have them stay standing for a few seconds, then invite them to sit back down.

One more question — Do you have a good friend that you know because of this church?

Almost everyone stands up.

Wow! That's a lot of people who made friends because of this church!

So let's get back to what we were wondering about earlier. Does going to church really matter? Look to the person on your right. Now look to the person on your left. It matters to them.

Of course God loves us and hears our prayers even when we're at home in our pjs. But there's only so much we can do by ourselves in our pjs. When we go to church we make friendships that last. When we go to church we're there for each other. When we go to church we can work together to do amazing things!

CLOSING

Everyone turn to a neighbor. Don't leave a single person out. Look your neighbor in the eye and say these words:

Hi, neighbor.
I love it when you're here,
And I miss you when you're gone.
You are a blessing to my life,
And a blessing to our church.
God bless our church,
And God bless you.
Amen.

WOLF

THEME
Tell the truth.

SCRIPTURE
Matthew 5:33-37 — You shall not swear falsely.

PREPARE
This children's moment centers around the re-telling of the classic fable of Aesop, "The Boy Who Cried Wolf." I love using Aesop's fables with kids. They're short, have engaging characters (often animals), and the lessons are usually very clear.

For our re-telling we had three sheep puppets and a wolf puppet, all operated by adult volunteers. The three sheep were all near the front of the worship space, and the wolf was stationed near the back, ready to enter at the appropriate time. If you don't have puppets, you could use stuffed animals, 3 headbands with wooly sheep ears and one headband with wolf's ears, or simply have adults pantomime the actions and make sounds of the animals. The idea here is to make the story come to life.

In the Moment
The Bible is full of many stories about shepherds and sheep. This story does not come from the Bible. Like so many great stories it starts with… *(Have the children say, "Once upon a time" with you.)*

Once upon a time, there was a shepherd who asked his son to watch over their flock of sheep. The boy was so excited. He felt very grownup to get to look after the sheep all by himself. So he went out into the meadow, and there were all the sheep.

Have the volunteers with the sheep hold them up for the kids to see.

He watched them as they ate grass. He watched them as they drank water. He watched them as they took naps. He watched, and watched…and watched, until it finally hit him — this is SO BORING!

So the boy decided he would do something to liven things up. At the top of his lungs he cried out, "Wolf, wolf, wolf!" Immediately all the villagers ran out to help the boy protect the sheep from the wolf. But when they reached the meadow, there was no wolf in sight, and the boy was laughing. He said, "You should have seen the looks on your faces! That was hilarious!" The villagers didn't think that was very funny. They all went back to what they were doing.

After a while, the boy got bored again. And he knew just what to do. Say it with me this time. The boy cried out, "Wolf, wolf, wolf!" Once again, all the villagers ran out to help the boy. And once again, there was no wolf, and the boy was laughing. The villagers all headed back to what they were doing. As they left they were grumbling about what should be done about boys who don't tell the truth.

After a while, something happened that wasn't boring at all — a wolf did show up.

Have the volunteer with the wolf puppet enter from the back.

As the wolf approached the sheep, the boy took one look and his knees started to shake. He tried to say, "W-w-w-w-olf," but he could hardly make a sound come out. Finally, with everything he had, he took in a deep breath and — say it with me — he cried out, "Wolf, wolf, wolf!"

Pause

And nobody came. Two times the boy had not told the truth when he cried, "Wolf." The villagers weren't coming to help. They didn't believe the boy. And so the wolf took the sheep.

Have the volunteers act this out. The wolf can gather the sheep all together at the front of the worship space, so that all four are in a row for the children to see.

But don't worry. The wolf did not eat the sheep. They formed a rock band called El Lobo and the Flufftones. They toured all over and even played at Caesar's Palace — the original Caesar's Palace. The sheep were gone, and the boy learned an important lesson about the importance of telling the truth.

CLosing
Invite the children to repeat after you each line of the following prayer.

Dear God,
We love you,
And we love your people.

One way we can show our love
Is by telling the truth.
Amen.

Hello in Many Languages

Theme

We don't have to speak the same language to understand how to reach out to one another in friendship.

Scripture

Acts 2:1-11 — The Coming of the Holy Spirit (Pentecost)

In the Moment

Let's practice saying hello in different languages.

Say *Hola*. *(The children say Hola.)* What language is that? *(A few children may answer, "Spanish.")* *Sí*. *Hola* is how you say hello in Spanish. Let's all say *Hola* one more time. *(The children say it again.)*

Now let's say *Jambo*. *(The children say Jambo.)* *Jambo* is how you say hello in Swahili, a language spoken in many countries in East Africa. Say *Jambo*. *(The children say Jambo.)*

Now let's say hello in Mandarin Chinese. Does anyone know how to do that? *(We have a child from China who is only too delighted to tell us Ni Hao.)* That's right, *Ni Hao*. Let's all practice that one together. *(The children say Ni Hao.)*

Very good. We've got one more. In Texas we have a special way to say hello — Howdy. Everyone say howdy. *(The children all say Howdy.)*

Okay, let's practice those one more time. *(Lead the children to say hello in English, Spanish, Swahili, Mandarin Chinese, and Texan.)*

That was wonderful. You're really good with different languages. Let's try something else.

Everyone smile in English. *(The children smile. They smile a lot, anyway.)* Now smile in Spanish. *(They smile. Some are confused. Some may even wonder aloud, "What's the difference?")*

Smile in Swahili. *(They smile.)* Smile in Mandarin Chinese. *(They smile again. Many are giggling.)* And finally, smile in Texan. *(They smile.)*

Okay, we're going to do something fun. I want you to think of your favorite language to say hello — hello, *hola, jambo, ni hao,* howdy, or even a different language — and I want you to say hello to three different people using the language you choose. By the way, feel free to smile in whatever language you choose.

Invite the adults to participate as well. The effect of a whole congregation saying hello in many languages at once is very powerful. The sound is amazing!

We don't all have to speak the same language to understand when words of kindness are being spoken. We don't all have to come from the same place to understand a smile. The important thing is that we keep trying to understand.

CLOSING
Invite the children to repeat after you each line of the following prayer.

God of many languages,
God of many lands,
Help us to look,
Help us to listen,
Help us to understand.
Amen.

PRiORiTY LiSt

THEME
What is most important to you?

SCRiPtURE
Luke 6:6-11 — Jesus Healing on the Sabbath

PREPARE
Provide a blank card and a crayon for each child. In our church this particular children's moment occurred on the morning of Halloween. So instead of a plain card, each child received a pumpkin card die-cut from orange cardstock. All the crayons were black.

In tHE MOMENt

I have to make a confession — I put off getting ready for this children's moment until it was too late. I wanted to do a children's moment on how to make a priority list. That's a list of things that matter to you, and the more important something is to you, the higher it goes on the list. But like I said I kept putting things off.

Three days ago I was all set to work on the children's moment...but there was a baseball game on TV I really wanted to see. I thought, "Well, if I watch the baseball game, I'll still have two more days. That should be enough time." So I watched the baseball game instead of working on this children's moment.

Two days ago, I was all set to work on the children's moment...but I saw the toys on my shelf, and I had the urge to put them in alphabetical order. Putting the toys in alphabetical order would make them easier to find. Well, it made sense at the time. And besides, I would still have another day to work on the children's moment. So I put my toys in alphabetical order.

Last night I was all set to work on the children's moment...but Gordon wouldn't stop staring at me. It was really distracting. I decided to stare back at Gordon until he blinked. He didn't blink. He never blinked. I should probably mention that Gordon is my pet gecko. Did you know that geckos don't have eyelids? In fact, since they don't blink, they lick their eyeballs to keep them moist. That looked really cool, so I spent the rest of the evening trying to lick my own eyeballs. Guess what? I can't! Not only that, but it was so late that I couldn't work on the children's moment.

So here we are, it's Sunday morning, and I haven't prepared the children's moment. I should really make a priority list so I can remember what is most important.

Take out one of the cards and a crayon.

I think I'll make a priority list right now so that next time I won't be stuck without a children's moment. Let's see — watch baseball, alphabetize my toys, stare at Gordon, work on the children's moment — that's four things. Well number 4 is alphabetizing my toys. *(Pretend to write each priority on the card — or actually write them down.)* As long as I put them away neatly, they don't have to be in alphabetical order.

Number 3 on my priority list will be…watching baseball. I like baseball, but it's not the most important thing.

So it's down to Gordon or the children. Hmm, I really like my pet gecko, Gordon. But…you children are more important. Creating the best children's moment I can will be my top priority.

I also have a card and a crayon for each of you. Today, right after church, I want you to think about the things that really matter to you, and write them down. If you want, you can draw pictures of your priorities instead of writing them. Keep your cards and look at them from time to time to help you remember what is most important.

Since we did this children's moment on Halloween morning, and the cards we used were pumpkin-shaped, I also suggested the kids decorate one side of their pumpkin cards however they wanted. That little bit of "permission" to do what many of the kids would want to do anyway with a pumpkin card, makes it a little more likely that they will do what I asked them to do on the other side.

CLOSING
Have the children repeat after you each line of the following prayer.

Dear God,
We've got our priorities.
We don't know what number 37 is.
We're not sure what number 14 is.
But we know what number 1 is.
It's you.
Amen.

Five Thousand

THEME
It's amazing what one simple act of sharing can mean for someone else.

SCRIPTURE
John 6:1-15 — Feeding the Five Thousand

In the Moment
This is one of the most inspirational stories in the whole Bible. It's about sharing, and I'm going to need your help. I'll tell the story, and I'll show you when to make some special sounds that really bring this story to life.

One day Jesus crossed the Sea of Galilee. *(Make vocal wind sounds.)* When he reached the other side, a huge crowd gathered to watch him cure the sick. *(Stomp in place to mimic the sound of moving feet.)* As the sun began to set, the disciples said, "It is getting late and these people have nothing to eat."*(Descending whistle or "loo" sound.)* "Then give them something to eat," Jesus replied. One of the disciples said to him, "There is a boy here who has five barley loaves and two fish. But what are they among so many people?"*(Clap five times. Make lip-pop sound twice.)*

Jesus said, "Make the people sit down." So the people, about five thousand in all, went to a grassy place and sat down. *(Rub hands together steadily to mimic the sound of walking through grass.)* Then Jesus took the loaves, and when he had given thanks, he broke the loaves and gave them to those who were seated. Then he did the same with the fish, as much as they wanted. *(Clap hands softly and continuously. Do the same with the lip-pops. Gradually get louder. Then all stop together.)* When the people were full, Jesus told his disciples to gather all the leftover pieces. The disciples gathered enough pieces to fill twelve baskets. *(Make "mmm" sounds.)*

CLOSING
Invite the children to repeat after you each line of the following poem prayer.

God is caring, God is kind —
Giving love and peace of mind.
We can follow God's own way
By sharing, caring every day.
Amen.

Hosanna

THEME
On Palm Sunday we celebrate having Jesus in our lives.

SCRIPTURE
Matthew 21:1-11 — Jesus' Triumphal Entry into Jerusalem

PREPARE
Many churches order palm branches for children to wave on Palm Sunday. This children's moment involves the waving of palm branches, but the waving could also be done simply using hands. (Distribute the palm branches to the children as they come forward for the children's moment.)

Also, if you have an organist or pianist, ask if he or she is willing to play the well-known musical intro that leads people at a sporting event to cheer, "Charge!"

In the Moment
Many of us have been to a sporting event like a baseball game or football game. We like to cheer for our team or our favorite player. The whole experience can be exciting, loud, and fun.

Why can't we bring that same excitement into worship? Having Jesus in our lives is every exciting, and something definitely worth celebrating. So let's celebrate!

Today is Palm Sunday. We're holding palm branches just like the children did when Jesus rode into Jerusalem. *(Many children are already waving their palm branches.)*

And as many of you can see, it's really hard to hold our palm branches still. Let's play a game. Everyone stand up and watch me very carefully. When I shake my palm branch, you shake yours. When I freeze, you freeze. And I will try to trick you, so watch carefully.

Play the game with the kids. Wave fast, slow, high, low – really mix it up. And freeze from time to time at unexpected intervals. The kids will really like this game. After a few rounds have the children sit down.

You know, watching you wave your palm branches reminds me of something we often do at a sporting event — The Wave. We're going to need the entire congregation to help with this. I'll start at one side, and we'll get the wave going all the way across the sanctuary. When it gets all the way across then the wave needs to come all the way back across the room. Ready? Here we go!

Start the wave, and encourage people to make the wave go all the way across the worship space and back again. You may need to do this a couple of times to get everyone involved. Some adults may simply refuse to participate. Oh well. Those who do will have a great time with the kids.

And on that great day when Jesus rode into Jerusalem, the people shouted, "Hosanna!" which means "save" or "help." It was their way of saying they believed in Jesus as their savior. We're going to clap along with our organist as he plays. Then at the right time, and you'll all know when that is, we'll shout "Hosanna!" Here we go.

The organist plays the steady intro that builds...and gets faster...until...nah-nah-nah-NAH-nah-NAH!

Hosanna!

nah-nah-nah-NAH-nah-NAH!

Hosanna!!!

nah-nah-nah-NAH-nah-NAH!

HOSANNA!!!

Jesus is in our hearts and in our lives, and that's exciting. That is something worth celebrating!

CLOSING
I'm going to say our prayer. Every time you hear me say the name *Jesus*, wave your palm branches in the air.

Thank you, God, for **Jesus**.
We are so excited to have **Jesus** in our lives.
And we are not afraid to celebrate **Jesus** with our whole hearts.
Amen.

SHE'S a HER♀

THEME
There are many women in the Bible who are great, not just because they are mothers or wives of great men, but because they are great in their own right.

SCRIPTURE
Various, including Genesis 18:9-15 — Sarah laughs; Judges 5 — The Song of Deborah; Esther; Luke 1:26-38 — An angel visits Mary; Acts 16:11-15 — Lydia.

In the Moment
Today we're going to think about heroes. The Bible is full of wonderful heroes. Now, they didn't wear a mask, or a cape, or fly an invisible plane, but they all had something that made them truly special. And they did things that we can do today. Let's look at some of these Bible heroes.

Invite the children to stand up.

Lydia was very smart. She was a wise businesswoman who dealt with purple cloth. And she was one of the earliest followers of the way of Jesus. We can have brains like Lydia.

Point to the side of your head as you say this to a steady beat.

Say it with me and do what I do.

Have the children join you in chanting, "Brains like Lydia."

Another hero of the Bible is Esther. She was very courageous and was able to save her people by speaking up when others would have been afraid to. We can have courage like Esther.

Pat chest as you say this. Then invite the children to say, "Courage like Esther," as they pat their chests.

Another hero is Mary. When an angel came and told her she would be the mother of Jesus, she had faith. She knew that if God trusted her with such an important role, she could do it. We can have faith like Mary.

Make praying hands as you say this to the steady beat. Then have the children do likewise.

Another hero is Deborah. She was great singer, not to mention a leader in battle. Deborah was strong! We can be strong like Deborah.

Make muscles as you say this to the steady beat. Then have the children do likewise.

And another hero is Sarah. She knew how to find the humor in a situation. She laughed when, as an old woman, she learned that she would become a mother. She became one of the most famous mothers in history. We can laugh like Sarah.

Hold your belly as you say this to the steady beat. Then have the children do this.

Does anyone know what all these heroes have in common? *(A few children may answer, "They're all women.")*

That's right, they're some of the *(say this part very dramatically)* Super Women of the Bible!!! They all did amazing things in their time, and they inspire us to be our best selves in our own time.

So the next time we open the Bible to read one of our favorite stories, let's not forget that all along the way women were a very important part of all of it!

CLOSING
Invite the children to repeat after you each line of the following poem prayer.

Women of the Bible,
They hold a special place,
They lead by their example,
They lead by strength and grace.
Amen.

Kazoos

THEME
God has created a wonderful world full of wonderful opportunities. What we get out of it depends on what we put of ourselves into it.

SCRIPTURE
Ephesians 3:20-21 — God's power at work within us

PREPARE
Acquire a plastic kazoo for each child. You may choose to recruit a few volunteers to help pass out the kazoos at the appropriate time.

In the Moment
I want to hear one of my favorite songs, "The More We Get Together," played on kazoo. And a one, and a two, and a three…*(Hold kazoo to your side while staring blankly for a few seconds.)*

Huh. Nothing. I guess if I want to hear "The More We Get Together" on kazoo, I better blow into the kazoo. Let's try that again. And a one, and a two, and a three…*(Blow air into the kazoo. No sound should come out. Merely blowing air through the kazoo won't make it sound much like a kazoo.)*

Oh, that's right. Just blowing air into the kazoo won't work. If I want to get a sound out of it, I've got to put a sound into it. Like this…

Sing an "oh" sound at a comfortable pitch. As you continue singing, place the wide end of the kazoo to your lips and sing the "oh" sound through the tube. This is your first demonstration of how to play the kazoo. You will most likely need to do this a few more times before the end of the children's moment.

There we go. That's how to play a kazoo. I have to put something into it to get something out of it. Now let me try this again.

Play "The More We Get Together" on the kazoo.

You know, that was pretty cool. But if one person putting himself into the music can sound pretty cool, a whole group of people putting themselves into the music would sound really cool. And guess what? We're about to find out because I've got kazoos for all of you!

Huge cheer. The volunteers help hand out the kazoos so this takes as little time as possible. Most of the kids will start playing their kazoos as soon as they get one in their hands. About half will have the small end of the kazoo in their mouths. Remind them that the wide end is the best, and that simply blowing won't produce a sound. Once all the children have a kazoo, continue.

Let's all practice. I'll play a few sounds and you echo me.

Make a game of it. Play a simple sequence of notes (two or three) and have the children echo the sequence back. Do this a few times.

Okay, that was the warm-up. Now let's all play "The More We Get Together"…together. And a one, and a two, and a three…(*Lead the children in playing the song on the kazoos.*)

That was great. It's amazing how much we get out of something when we truly put something of ourselves into it.

Cʟᴏsɪɴɢ
The kids have kazoos. Any chance for a quiet closing prayer is off the table. Might as well integrate kazoo playing into the closing. Sing or chant the following prayer. Have the children echo each line through their kazoos.

With our whole hearts
We can give praise
To you, O Lord.
Amen, amen, amen.

W. I. T. H.

THEME
There are many kinds of prayers — Wow prayers, I'm Sorry prayers, Thank You prayers, Help prayers. Every time we pray, we are acknowledging that God is W.I.T.H. us every step of the way.

SCRIPTURE
Luke 11:1-4 — Teach Us How to Pray

PREPARE
Use cardstock to make four signs, each with one of the following letters — W – I – T – H. Get four adult volunteers who will sit with the four signs in the worship space (make sure they sit in the order of the word). Have each volunteer stand up and show his or her letter when it is called out by the children.

In the Moment
Today we are going to explore prayer. Praying means talking with God, and there are many ways we can pray, many things we can say. First let's get a drum roll going. *(Lead the children to "drum roll" by having then rapidly pat their knees.)* As you drum roll, listen carefully. I'm going to say, "Give me a letter," and I want you to say that letter nice and loud. Get ready, here we go. Give me a "W"! *(The children yell "W" and the volunteer holding the W sign stands up.)*

Look there's even a W here in the worship space. W stands for the word "Wow." God created this amazing world we live in. Sometimes we need to stop, look around, and simply say "Wow." I want you to put on your thinking caps. *(Invite the children to do this. It's a lot more fun than simply asking them to think about something.)* Think about your favorite animal in the whole world. Think about how that animal looks and what it can do. Now offer the simple one-word prayer by telling God, "Wow!" *(Indicate for the children to call out "Wow!")*

Okay, let's get another drum roll going. *(Have the children drum roll.)* Give me an "I!" *(The children yell "I" and the volunteer holding the I sign stands up next to the volunteer with the W.)* The I stands for "I'm sorry." We all make mistakes from time to time. And as my Nana says, "Fess up when you mess up." When we mess up, we can say "I'm sorry" to God. Put your thinking caps back on. I want you to think of a time when you've really messed up and done something you know you shouldn't have. Now I want you to think the words, "I'm sorry." You don't have to say it out loud. This is between you and God. *(Allow the children a moment.)*

It's time for another drum roll. *(Have the children drum roll again.)* Give me a "T!" *(The children yell "T" and the volunteer holding the T sign stands. The children get excited each time a new letter "pops" up.)* The T stands for "Thank you." God has given us so many blessings. And sometimes the best prayer we can offer is simply, "Thank you." Okay, time for those thinking caps again. Think about something wonderful, like a loving family member or a dear friend that you have because of God. Let's all say "Thank you" together. *(Have the children say "Thank you" together.)*

One more drum roll, here we go! *(Have the children drum roll one more time.)* Give me an "H!" *(The children yell "H" and the volunteer holding the H sign stands.)* The H stands for "Help." No matter how smart we are, no matter how big we get, we still need help sometimes. And there are plenty of times when others need help. Let's put on our thinking caps one more time and think of something we could use help with. Or maybe we can think of someone else who needs help. Now let's pray to God, the one who always listens when we and others need help. *(Give the children a moment to think of a time when they or another could use some help. Then have them all say "Help" together.)*

Did you notice? The first letter for each of our prayers spells the word W.I.T.H. We can talk with God anytime, day or night. Every step of the way, God is there to listen to us and love us. God is always with us.

CLOSING
Have the children repeat after you each line of the following prayer.

Dear God,
Thank you for being W.I.T.H. us
Every step of the way.
Amen.

BY THE WAY
I did this children's moment on Father's Day. So, in honor of the dads, I made the letters on the card stock signs using torn strips of duct tape. (Is there anything duct tape can't do?)

SCRIPTURE INDEX

Genesis 1:1-31; 2:1-4 44
Genesis 3:1-24................................50
Genesis 12; 17; 18; and 21 25
Genesis 18:9-15..............................106
Genesis 50:20.................................65
Judges 5...106
Ruth 1:16..86
1 Samuel 10:6-7 23
1 Kings 19:1-18 46
Esther 106
Psalm 139:13-14.............................16
Proverbs 20:11 69
Ecclesiastes 4:9 88
Isaiah 2:4 65
Isaiah 11:6-9 69
Isaiah 35:1-10 75
Isaiah 66:13 33
Matthew 2:1-12.......................52, 73
Matthew 5:33-37...........................97
Matthew 19:21 90
Matthew 21:1-11............................104
Matthew 28:16-20..........................28
Mark 1:9-11....................................91
Mark 16:1-8 37
Luke 1:26-38 106
Luke 2:1-7 71
Luke 2:1-20 52
Luke 5:1-11 49
Luke 6:6-11 101
Luke 9:48...30
Luke 10:25-37 18
Luke 11:1-4 110
Luke 22:19.......................................59
Luke 24:13-35 47
John 6:1-15 103
John 6:25-35 56
John 8:12..54
John 10:1-4 14

John 10:1-10 42
John 11:32-37 84
John 14:1-7 40
John 20:19-22 80
John 20:19-29 35
Acts 1:1-8 31
Acts 2:1-11......................................99
Acts 6:1-7 48
Acts 16:11-15 106
Acts 16:16-40..................................63
Romans 8:25 93
1 Corinthians 12:14-20....................12
1 Corinthians 13:1-13.....................61
Ephesians 3:20-21 108
Colossians 4:3..................................20
2 Timothy 3:16-17 82
Hebrews 11:1....................................77
James 1:22 10
1 Peter 2:10......................................95
1 Peter 3:15-16 67
Revelation 3:8 20
Revelation 21:5................................16